Decide for Peace

Decide for Peace:
Evangelicals and the Bomb

Compiled by Evangelical Peacemakers

edited by Dana Mills-Powell

MARSHALL PICKERING

For Jim

Marshall Morgan and Scott
Marshall Pickering
3 Beggarwood Lane, Basingstoke, Hants RG23 7LP, UK

First published in 1986 by Marshall Morgan and Scott
(Publications) Ltd
Part of the Marshall Pickering Holdings Group
A subsidiary of the Zondervan Corporation

ISBN: 0 551 013737
Phototypeset in Linotron Bembo 11 on 12pt
by Input Typesetting Ltd, London

Printed in Great Britain by Camelot Press Ltd,
Southampton, Hants

Contents

Editor's Preface

Life seems to go on undisturbed even during the editing of a book such as the one you are holding. In the months that these chapters were compiled, Mr. Gorbachev and Mr. Reagan met for the first time, four urban areas in Britain erupted in violence, and – putting all these events in their place – our first child was born. Bridget provided us with an important counterpoint of hope, both to world events and to many of the more dismal facts included in this book.

The chapters of this book came from many different sources. As many of them were originally sermons, seminar notes, or meditations, they reflect more than simply the convictions of the authors. Rather, they come out of the life of congregations, groups, or conferences to which these words were first given. They represent a growing movement among evangelicals in Britain.

Drawing these contributions from such various sources in the evangelical community would necessarily result in much over-lapping of material. Instead of attempting to restrict points of argument to one appearance only, we feel their repetition throughout the book will be helpful as the significance will vary according to the context of each chapter.

Although this book is compiled under the auspices of Evangelical Peacemakers, a network of Christians opposed to nuclear weapons, not all the authors are formally associated with the group. Therefore, there will be material in the book which neither others in the network nor the other authors would express in the same way. But differing emphasis and argument, we believe, will strengthen the overall picture.

In order to be faithful to God's challenge for both men and women to be responsible for creation, I have changed pronouns and nouns to reflect the inclusive nature of our calling as Christian people. I ask for your patience wherever the text is slightly cumbersome.

Many thanks must go to several people who provided essential services to the completion of this book. Julia Pierce, Sheila Thomas, and Barbara Stevens selflessly gave hours over to the typing and transcription of several of these chapters. Nancy Coyle and Jean Hewitt cared for Bridget. Members of the 'Theological Support Group' of Evangelical Peacemakers provided the necessary oversight for the project, and Debbie Thorpe of Marshall Pickering, the vision for the potential contribution it might make. Mark Mills-Powell helped provide a creative and loving environment in which to work.

Dana Mills-Powell
Liverpool
November 1985.

Foreword

The sixteen contributors to this symposium come from many different backgrounds. They include a university professor, a suffragan bishop, several theological teachers, several local church pastors, an ex-publisher, a mother, a race relations worker and a youth worker. They also adopt different positions in relation to the legitimacy of force and the complexities of disarmament.

Yet at least three factors unite them. First, they are all evangelical Christians who are resolved to submit to the lordship of Christ, and so to the authority of Scripture which he endorsed. Most of the book's chapters are, in fact, biblical studies. Secondly, the authors are the kind of evangelical Christians who have repented of the old pietism, which previously held sway among us, and which emphasized personal commitment at the expense of social involvement. Instead, these writers are struggling to relate God's Word to the harsh and horrific realities of contemporary nuclear arsenals. Their particular concerns lead them also to write of peace in relation to other realities such as world hunger, racism, the deprivations of the inner city, stewardship of the environment and the need for spiritual revival. Thirdly, the authors of this book glow with passion. They make no attempt to hide the deep feelings which their topic stirs within them.

My own mind on this matter has changed over the years. Converted to Jesus Christ in my later teens, shortly before the outbreak of World War II, I would describe myself at that time as an instinctive pacifist. Having read the Sermon

on the Mount thoughtfully for the first time, it seemed to
me self-evident that Jesus' prohibition of retaliation carried
with it a ban on all participation in war. But as I learned
to compare Scripture with Scripture, the issue became less
clearcut for me. It was a careful study of Romans 12:17–13:5
which convinced me of the state's God-given authority to
punish evildoers, and to use force in doing so. This led me
to resign from the Anglican Pacifist Fellowship. But then
came the development and proliferation of nuclear weapons,
which I found myself unable to fit into the categories of just
war thinking which I had accepted. My conscience
condemned both the indiscriminate use of conventional
weapons (as in the blanket bombing of German cities) and
all use of indiscriminate weapons (chemical and biological as
well as nuclear). For these things contradict Scripture, which
forbids the shedding of innocent blood. They infringe the
just war principles of control and proportion, as well as of
discrimination. And they have been outlawed by common
consent in the Hague Convention and the Geneva Protocol.
When Scripture, tradition and common sense are united in
their condemnation of something, the case is overwhelming.

Conviction and passion are not enough, however. The
contributors to this symposium call for prayer and agitation
on behalf of peace. The groundswell of opposition to nuclear
missiles is growing. The fundamental incompatibility of
weapons of mass destruction with the justice and peace of
the Kingdom of God is increasingly perceived. Now what
is needed is a programme. Perhaps 'Evangelical Peacemakers'
will seek to develop one. Although it is essential to *Decide
for Peace*, our decision has to be translated into action.

John Stott
April 1986

Michael Green

For some of us, a conviction about peace comes suddenly and unexpectedly; a case in point is our first author, Michael Green. Michael, a well-known Christian writer and preacher, and also rector of St. Aldate's, Oxford, was preparing his Christmas sermon a few years ago, and came upon a verse he'd read countless times, but had never struck him in the way it did that day. '. . . Christ Jesus, who, though he was in the form of God, did not count equality with God a thing to be grasped, but emptied himself, taking the form of a servant, being born in the likeness of men.' (Phil:2.6–7) That an all-powerful God should become one of us, while we strive for ultimate power to destroy was too much of a contradiction. Canon Green has become more and more outspoken in his conviction that nuclear weapons are a hideous testament to human sin, especially in the light of a God who unilaterally disarmed Himself.

Michael's chapter is adapted from a sermon preached at St. Aldate's on 24 June 1984.

1: Hope in a Nuclear World

Michael Green

What hope is there in a nuclear world? When Peter wrote the words that follow, it must have all looked very speculative.

'The heavens and the earth that now exist have been stored up for fire, being kept until the day of judgement and destruction of ungodly men. But the day of the Lord Will come like a thief, and then the heavens will pass away with a loud noise, and the elements will be dissolved with fire, and the earth and the works that are upon it will be burned up.' (2 Peter 3:7, 10)

Since the atom bomb was released on Hiroshima, an irreversible possibility of global destruction has become the daily backcloth of our world. President Kennedy, during the Cuban missile crisis, placed the danger of global destruction at somewhere between 30–50% chance probability. President Carter said, 'All countries must find ways to control and reduce the horrifying danger that is posed by the world's stock-pile of nuclear arms. It may only be a matter of time before madness, desperation, greed, or miscalculation lets loose this terrifying force.'

President Carter also said that in an all-out war, more destructive power than in all of World War II would be unleashed every second for the long afternoon it would take for all the missiles to fall. Of course, the idea of a limited tactical war with nuclear weapons is naive – rather it would

be a World War II every second. More people would be
killed in the first few hours than in all the wars of history
put together. The survivors, if any, would live in despair
among the poisoned ruins of a civilisation that had
committed suicide. So spoke the man who had the power
to bring this about, the President of the United States.

Billy Graham, when he went to visit Auschwitz, the scene
of the ghastly holocaust perpetrated by the Nazis on the Jews
in World War II, said:

'Is nuclear holocaust inevitable if the arms race is not
stopped? Frankly, the answer is almost certainly yes. Some
people feel human beings are so terrified of a nuclear war
that nobody would ever dare start one. I wish I could
accept that, but neither history nor the Bible gives much
room for such optimism. The present intensity of the arms
race, if continued, will lead inevitably to a conflagration
so great that Auschwitz will seem like a minor rehearsal.'

What I have to say can be divided into three parts. First,
I want to examine the situation that we all have to face,
whether we like it or not, for the United Kingdom has the
greatest density per square mile of nuclear weaponry of any
country in the world.

Second, I want to look at the alternatives that are put
before us in the face of this horrifying situation. Third, I
want to see how this passage in 2 Peter 3 encourages us to
live in the light of possible global catastrophe.

The Nuclear Backdrop

Nuclear fission is cheap and vastly more powerful than
conventional methods of producing power. That's why it is
so attractive for commercial as well as for military purposes.
But consider some of the probable, or certain, consequences.
I outline seven.

First there is the danger of radioactivity coming from the
processing plants. 'Silkwood' is a moving film on this
subject, and we all know the prevalence of cancer in the
whole area around the Windscale experiment.

Secondly, radiation in the atmosphere coming from nuclear weapons programmes built up over 30 years. Recently it has been realised that British tests, in the Montebello Islands off Australia in the South Pacific which took place in 1956, but which were comparatively small, are now having appalling continued effects upon life.

Third, there is the possibility of human error unleashing a nuclear attack, and this danger is increasing all the time. Fourth, there is the proliferation of nuclear waste. The Ashby Report said soberly, 'We are consciously and deliberately accumulating a very toxic substance on the off-chance that it may be possible to get rid of it at a later date.'

Fifth, consider the possibility of nuclear terrorism and hijacking. What if Colonel Gaddafy gets hold of a nuclear bomb? Sixth, consider what an offence to God, God our Creator, is afforded by this constant build-up of arms for global destruction. The United Kingdom is one of the world's biggest arms retailers and 80% of those arms go to Third World countries, where more is spent on weaponry than on health and education combined. While the resources of these poor countries are squandered in this way, 12 million of their children die each year of hunger and ten million refugees wander around the world. What does God think about that?

The seventh consideration is this terrifying statistic: over 50% of the world's top physicists and engineers are engaged in research for military ends, most of which is for nuclear programmes. Just think what a blessing it would be to the world if that amount of brilliant inventiveness, and the technology that flows from it, were harnessed to genuinely peaceful purposes. Politicians, of course, fear that there would be a loss of jobs in armament factories if there were to be a change. But those men and women could be employed, if the political will was there, to meet human need and extend trade.

On top of these seven considerations, there is the ever-present fear of nuclear war. Such are the appalling shadows cast by the approaching nuclear winter. They constitute the most serious problem humankind has ever had to face and that is why I am so concerned.

Alternatives

There are two main approaches taken by those who want peace and Christians are to be found adopting both of these. One is reliance on deterrence. The argument runs that there must be a 'balance of terror' for multilateral disarmament to be agreed. This is the way adopted by the NATO countries by and large, and by our government in particular. Deterrence, it is claimed, has kept the peace for nearly forty years. It is the best card we have in a weak hand.

There are strong arguments in favour of this stance. It makes good sense if the other side has the power, then we've got to have it too. Whatever dreams Russia may have of world sovereignty and her actual conventional military superiority presents the challenge to which we need some powerful counterpoise. It is cheaper to finance nuclear arms than conventional, so that seems the best way to keep peace in a broken world.

That is the received wisdom in this country at the moment. And yet four uncomfortable questions rear their heads. First, does the balance of terror not inevitably lead to an escalation in the arms race? The replacement of Polaris by Trident, which we are told, is just a new car for an old, is no mere modernization, but a 14-factor strengthening. It provides an arsenal of 896 nuclear warheads for this country instead of 64. Such an increase in accuracy and destructive capacity means that we can actually pick off the Russian weapon silos like sitting ducks. Is it any wonder that the Russians are nervous?

The second question that I can't escape from is this: does escalation between the superpowers not inevitably make peace less likely and increase the chances of holocaust? The Chief of Defence Staff, Field Marshall Lord Carver, rightly protested, 'NATO cannot stake the whole future on a strategy which is either a bluff or a suicide pact.'

Third, does the idea of the just war, that has long been given reluctant assent by Christian thinkers, make sense any more in the context of a nuclear exchange? Can you have retribution which is proportional and discriminatory? No, of course you can't. John Stott therefore said, 'Every Christian, whatever he may think of the just use of conventional weapons, must be a nuclear pacifist.' Mutually Assured Destruction, MAD, as it is called, is mad indeed, and we need not be embarrassed to say so.

The fourth question: can you imagine Jesus either using nuclear arms or threatening to do so? That is a determinative question for those who claim to be disciples of Jesus. And there, of course, is the rub for the Christian. Because if the *action* is wrong, so must the *threat* be wrong, for it would be no deterrent unless you were willing, if the worst happened, to press the button. One of the most amazing men I have ever met is Harold Hughes. Harold Hughes was a drunk, alcoholic truck driver in the United States. He was saved by Christ and his potential began to be developed. He became a Senator and then ran for the Presidency in 1972. He was doing well in the primary elections, but he pulled out. Why? Because, he said, that as a Christian, 'I could never bring myself to press that button. My Master could not do it.'

There is an alternative strategy. It is to totally renounce nuclear arms. The aim of those who take this approach is that there should first be a freeze, then a commitment not to use nuclear weapons under any circumstances, and then to destroy them. The unilateralist position also adds that if the other side declines to do it first, then I will do it. There's the risk. It seems utter madness in a world that is bristling with nuclear arms, but is it? Several questions challenge thoughtful Christians on this matter:

● Can a Christian ever say without qualification 'my country, right or wrong'? Has he not got a higher allegiance?
● Is democracy so important to God that we should risk destroying the world in order to defend it?
● Are there no holds barred in pursuit of a just cause? Is nothing forbidden when you are striving for justice – even mutual destruction?
● Did God exert His titanic power upon us, His creatures, or did He lay it aside at the Incarnation and become totally vulnerable and suffer the consequences of that vulnerability upon the cross? Yet that cross, the symbol of shame, weak-

ness, and defeat, has become the greatest moral power in the world to change hate into love and suspicion into trust. Dare we take the same path?

● When there is a stalemate, does not someone have to take the first step in becoming vulnerable? If it is someone, should it not be those who can say they believe in God Almighty, Creator and Saviour?

● What if it doesn't work? What if we abjure arms and are over-run by an enemy? That would be a terrible thing, but does not the experience of Christianity in Russia and China show how indestructable the faith of Jesus is? It is like an oak tree on the exposed slopes of a Welsh mountain, flourishing in winter.

● Is not the whole thrust of Israelite policy in the Old Testament to trust in the armaments of the superpowers, Egypt on the one hand, or Assyria on the other? And is not the whole thrust of the prophets a call to abandon such sterile dependence on arms, and to trust, foolishly it would seem, in the living God? Has that Old Testament paradigm anything to say to us today?

Whichever way we choose, I would plead that those who are Christian would allow the example of Jesus, faith in God, and the teaching of the Scriptures – not the political slogans of the politicians – to determine your thinking, acting, and discussing in these matters. General Bradley said, 'We have grasped the mystery of the atom and we have rejected the Sermon on the Mount.' Don't let's do that. Today the hands of the nuclear clock stand at a few minutes to midnight, and, as Martin Luther King observed, the choice is no longer between violence and nonviolence: it is between nonviolence and non-existence. What might it look like if we began down that other road, the road of forebearance and forgiveness? That road starts in the human heart. It's to be found in the home, it spreads into society, it could embrace the whole planet.

The Other Road

Because the people to whom Peter wrote 2 Peter 3 were not expecting the world to go on unchanged for ever, as we blandly do, they believed that cosmic destruction was possible. In verse six, they looked back to when life had perished through the flood; why should it not, as it says in verse seven, perish in the future by fire? So Peter gives practical advice to these ordinary believers, who were little people much like us, and not able to alter greatly the pattern of events. We too could well profit from his advice.

There are six things here for us. First, verse ten, on Christian hope: 'The day of the Lord will come like a thief' – when you least expect it (3:10). History is not ultimately moving on to chaos, so Scripture claims, but it is moving on to Christ. History is His story. The Lord made this earth, the Lord came on this earth, the Lord will return at the end of history. That is the concerted teaching of the scriptures. Whether we must go through nuclear fire to get there, as this passage seems to indicate, we cannot say.

There were strident warnings to Nineveh in the Old Testament and yet the doom of Nineveh was averted by repentance. Whether or not we have to go through nuclear fire, the last word does not lie with the bomb, but with the Lord. The Lord God omnipotent is reigning; that is the message of the book of Revelation to people who lived in apocalyptic times under a totalitarian regime with an Emperor who was totally unpredictable and who had a deep hatred for Christ. Wars and rumours of wars were to be found everywhere, and the book of Revelation reflects them.

But every now and again, the Christians seem to get a glimpse into God's throne room and they say 'There is the Lamb that was slain sitting on the throne, the Lord God omnipotent is reigning.' In the beginning God; at the end, God. And even down the course of history, behind the scenes, He holds the strands, He is in control. Is there any hope in a nuclear age? Yes, there is one hope only; the Living God. Get clear on your hope.

Second, be ready to meet your God. 'Seeing all these things are thus to be dissolved, what sort of persons ought you to be?' (3:11). It may be you will meet God at his return, if the climax of all history happens in our lifetime. It may be at your death. But this is an appointment which we must all keep. There will be no latecomers, there will be no absentees on that day. Are you ready to meet your God? If so, you'll be free to live. If not, it is crucial to get right with Him speedily. Be ready to meet your God.

Third, love your enemies. Verse nine reads, 'The Lord is not slow about his promise, as some count slowness.' Why hasn't He come again? Because He is forbearing towards you, not wishing that any should perish, but that all should come to repentance.' The Lord loves his rebel subjects (indeed St. Paul calls them his enemies) so much that he not only died to draw them to Himself, but in patient, humble love waits for them to return. Such is our God! And if that is what He is like, should not our attitude be the same? Love your enemies, do not annihilate them. And just as the Lord is longing for them to change their minds and repent, so we must encourage them in the same direction. Therefore, get involved in evangelism, in calling the rebel subjects back to their Lord. Love your enemies – and of course, the best way to love them is to introduce them to the Great Lover.

Fourth, live a holy, godly life. 'Since all these things are to be dissolved, what sort of persons ought you to be, in lives of holiness and godliness, waiting for and hastening the coming of the Day of the Lord.' (3:11). Sometimes both the nuclear and the anti-nuclear lobbies have a stridency, almost a bitterness which is very alien from the peace which they profess they want to keep. Peacefulness in the home, peacefulness in the heart, peacefulness in the committee, peacefulness at work, is vital for those who would set up as peacemakers on a wider front. This emphasis on godliness is arresting. God lived a life like ours; He came amongst us and He shared in it in Jesus Christ and now He calls us to live a life like God: 'godliness'. The way we do that is to ask all the time, 'What would Jesus do if He was in my shoes?' After all, he did come into our shoes! So what would He do if He was here now?

Fifth, look for peace and work for it. Verse 13 maintains that, 'according to his promise we wait for a new heaven and a new earth in which righteousness dwells.' Scripture makes it plain that humanity's attempts to create peace are no more than a tower of Babel. God alone can prevail to usher in peace, but we need to be looking that way. We need to be working that way even though we know that our efforts are, at best, provisional. We should always be found straining for peace, that new heaven and that new earth. We should be peacemakers in our world – we should be pressing upon government and in every forum of public debate consideration of this most crucial issue for the future of the human race. History shows that many of those who have been the most successful reformers on earth have been inspired by a vision of the new heaven and the new earth in which righteousness dwells. May we belong to them.

The sixth thing I see here is the need to trust in God more and more. 'You therefore, beloved, knowing this beforehand, beware lest you be carried away with the error of lawless men and lose your own stability' (3:17). Christians know it is an unstable world; but our God reigns, and our Lord Jesus Christ will return. 'Therefore beloved, be zealous to be found in Him without spot and blemish and at peace' (3:14). There is a place of utter calm in the eye of the storm, and that is the place for the Christian to abide, that's where peace and hope are to be found. It is as you and I abide in Christ, keeping close to Him and experiencing His strength and knowing His person, that we will grow in the grace and knowledge of our Lord Jesus Christ (3:18).

I close with a story about Archbishop Helder Camara who is the leading Brazilian advocate of nonviolence, a Roman Catholic leader of great courage. His house has been machine-gunned and his life threatened a great many times. He tells us that sure hope belongs to those who follow Jesus, in His cross-bearing and in His way of love. Very often he says, 'I am questioned about living here all alone, especially during the night, opening the door myself to all callers. "It would be so easy to be killed," they say. My answer is always the same: "But I do not live here by myself. There are three other persons here, the Father, the Son and the Holy Spirit. See how I am protected!" ' That is true for a country as well as for an individual. No wonder Peter concludes his letter with a paean of praise to his Lord and Protector: 'To Him be glory both now and to the day of eternity. Amen.'

Peter Hall

The Rt. Rev. Peter Hall was instituted as Bishop of Woolwich in the Diocese of Southwark in November 1984. Prior to this he lived in Birmingham where he served as Rector of St. Martin's-in-the-Bull Ring (Birmingham Parish Church). He has been chairman of the Evangelical Coalition for Urban Mission and is a member of the 'Theological Support Group' of Evangelical Peacemakers.

In this chapter, Peter shows how a serious commitment to evangelical theology propels one into an active witness for peace. Noting that evangelicals have defined the potential impact of the gospel narrowly, he calls for a renewed understanding of the corporate aspects of Christ's challenge to us.

This is an adapted version of his keynote address at the Evangelical Peacemakers' third national gathering, November 1985.

2: Evangelical Truths for Peacemakers

Peter Hall

As evangelicals, we emphasize and hold dear certain doctrines which are very important in undergirding and understanding the call of God upon us to stand for peace in today's world. Four of those particular theological concerns I want to examine in some detail in this article. Firstly, as evangelicals we hold very firmly to the need for repentance of sin, and that Christ died for our sins. We also believe that the only way out of that particular destructive and tragic state is His offer of salvation to us. That doctrine of sin, which lies right at the heart of evangelical belief and practice, impinges strongly on the question of peace.

From our understanding of sin, there has been no feasible way to disarm people without opening the door to some other form of exploitation and violence . . . because we are sinners. Professor Herbert Butterfield gave a series of lectures following the Second World War, called 'Christianity and History', positing the classic problem of disarmament. There are two people in a room, each armed with a revolver. How do they, without any kind of trust in each other, actually get rid of their revolvers? He explores all the things they might do with them, all of which fail. The only possible answer to the problem is that some third person should come and remove the two revolvers.

There is a very real problem here which touches every level of human political life. For instance, recently I have been serving as an independent chairman of negotiations between a local authority and the police. We are trying to set up a consultative committee that might be useful in the present situation of mistrust between the public and police. I have been aware of standing between two power blocks, so to speak, just waiting for one of them to give ground a little for negotiation. But I know that neither of them is going to make any compromise until the last possible moment when they think perhaps everything's going to fall apart if they don't.

That is just an example of the all-pervading hard reality that every one of us has to face. But it is quite another thing to argue (as it often is), that because of this understanding of the doctrine of sin – that all human beings are infected in this way – that it would be totally unrealistic today to talk about initiating processes of disarmament. The new nuclear situation has made a radical difference to that particular argument. I quote from a letter from a group called 'Clergy Against Nuclear Arms': 'Nuclear weapons are by their very nature indiscriminate: in space, because their effects are spread over a wide area; in time, because some of those effects will be felt by unborn generations; in menace, because of the unacceptably high probability that any nuclear war will spread out of control.'

The moment we get into the totally indiscriminate use of weapons, the whole direction of the argument begins to change. Therefore, we find that the doctrine of sin is leading us to quite a different perception. The doctrine raises the question about where evil is primarily located. Our understanding of sin is very straightforward. Let's imagine that you were to step into a space vehicle and travel off to some far corner of the universe and land on a planet where conditions of life were perfect. There were already living creatures there who had never been infected by 'The Fall'. But trouble would begin in that world the moment you, or I, landed! Everything from that point would go wrong, because the problem, as the doctrine makes clear, is located within each of us.

Therefore, it is impossible (with that understanding of sin) to try to locate the problem somewhere other than ourselves, especially in some other group of people who, if they were wiped out, it is suggested would save the world a lot of bother. Romans 3 sets out very clearly the universality of sin (quoting from the Old Testament): 'There is no just man, not one, no one who understands, no one who seeks God. All have swerved aside, all alike have become debased'. (vv. 11 and 12). Then in verse 23, Paul summarises, 'All alike have sinned and have come short of the glory of God'. That's where we stand, and the consequence is that problems can't be solved by wiping out whole nations, because sin will remain.

We find that doctrine, therefore, is pointing us in this direction – to the folly of trying to solve human problems by straightening 'Them' out. This is one of the realisations that I've had hammered into my head again in becoming a bishop! I always knew that clergy were very slippery people, especially as I am one myself! I've now discovered even more sharply how true it is! One of the things that clergy do in the Church of England – (I'm sure those in other churches must handle things in different ways!) – is to get rid of a whole lot of problems by blaming 'Them' . . . namely, of course, the hierarchy, the bishops. Now I can recognise the process that is going on, but I know also that it is a very real human need to have 'Them' to blame. I've done it all my life. We all do it, whether in church life or in any human organisation. But our understanding of sin says 'It is within us all, that is where the problem lies,' and blaming or destroying 'Them' is not actually going to help to solve the problems of the human race.

Till he comes again

Secondly, we also hold very dear, as evangelicals, the doctrine of the Second Coming of Christ. I think the Second Coming has been used by some evangelical Christians as a cause for welcoming the possibility of nuclear war through a nightmarish piece of logic. Having identified nuclear war as being the means of the Second Coming, and Christians having always been taught to welcome the Second Coming, nuclear war then is a thing not to be worried about, but even to be positively welcomed! There are passages, of course, such as in Mark 13 vv. 24–26, where references to the Second Coming, using physical symbols, could be applied to the kind of conditions that would come in a nuclear holocaust.

That attitude is a total distortion of what we are told by Jesus about obedience in the light of the Second Coming. He tells many parables about it, and they give a very clear picture of what is important about it for us. For instance, in Luke 12:15 is the parable about the unsatisfactory servant, who, when left to deal with things in the master's absence, fails to do so, and is found dealing unjustly with those under his authority. This teaching about the Second Coming, like others which frequently end with words like 'watch' and 'be vigilant', is clearly a teaching about stewardship. It's a teaching about how we handle what God has given us, so that it can be presented to Him at the moment He comes. When I was making a proposal in the Birmingham Anglican Diocesan Synod about nuclear weapons, I had a letter just beforehand from a lady who pointed out something that I had never noticed. Jesus, while looking at the Temple, said 'Not one stone will stand on another here. This place is due for destruction'. Yet, within a very short time of saying that, He marched into the Temple and cleared it of all those who were defacing it and profaning it by their profit-making. Simply because it was going to be destroyed did not mean that Jesus would lose His passion for His stewardship of God's house. The fact that it only had a short time before its destruction did not cause Jesus to neglect to care for it, until it was to be handed back to God at the end of its time. It follows then, that the fact that this world is due to be dissolved in favour of the new heavens and the new earth, is no ground whatsoever for any lack of proper stewarding of God's world.

Stewardship must take account of two areas of concern. We must care for the planet for generations to come, for animal life, for vegetable life, and for human life. There is now evidence of a potential famine that would ensue from a nuclear war, in addition to the long-term, ecological effects, creating the impossibility for any life anywhere on this planet

because of all that would change as a result of such a disturb-
ance in its whole balance.

There is also a stewardship of human life now. The other
aspect of the arms race is the deflection of resources that
might be used for the improvement of human life which for
millions is lived in sub-human conditions. This aspect of
stewardship we find in Jesus' parable in Matthew 25:31–46,
which asks awkward questions like 'When I was poor, when
I was sick, when I was naked, when I was in prison, when
I was hungry, did you try to meet my need?' The moment
we appear before the King, those are the questions that
will be asked. How could you steward your world with its
starving masses when you were busy building up the nuclear
arsenals?

Under His Lordship

Thirdly, the doctrine of the Lordship of Christ, which
again is dear to the heart of evangelicals, has many implications for us in facing the need for peace in our world. The
implications are not only for us as individuals, but also for
us in a corporate sense. It requires that each person allow
Christ in their lives to become Lord, and then all parts of
one's personality will be brought under that Lordship. That's
a lifetime's job, and we call it sanctification. But Lordship
is also an issue that has to do with the Kingdom of God,
which pertains to the public and corporate areas of life in
this world, as well as in my individual life.

Jesus often attacked corporate realities in the New Testament in a way that we've interpreted as being directed solely
to the individual. In Matthew 23, he criticises right the way
through the religious authorities, the scribes and Pharisees.
The attack is so awesome that it caused a Jewish friend of
mine once to ask me to find one nice thing that Jesus said
to a Pharisee. Of course, Pharisees were some of the best
people of their time to whom one didn't want to have to
say repeatedly 'Woe!' What Jesus was actually attacking was
not a group of individuals, but rather a corporate system of
life, the theocratic understanding of a nation-state which had
become oppressive. It was functioning in such a way that

those who were setting the rules of the system were unaware of the impact upon those who were under its weight. We've misunderstood many of the things that Jesus taught us because we've not seen that he was dealing with public, corporate realities. The crucifixion was a product of such corporate realities. The Roman Empire produced the best system of human justice the world had known, and the religion of the Jewish people had the clearest understanding of God's righteousness. Yet those two things combined to do a terribly unjust and unrighteous thing. It was also done with the will of the people, something which we now call democracy and value above almost all else. Corporate factors were at work in Jesus' crucifixion, distorted by sin.

So what does the Lordship of Christ mean for these corporate realities? It means that they have to be identified, and clearly put under His Lordship, no longer having any absolute claim or power of their own, because they are secondary to Him. Corporate realities in our world try to claim us absolutely. They try to lay upon us ultimate claims that only belong to Christ. They are not done away with, but they have their place. For example, nationhood will try to claim absolutely the loyalty, and belonging, and the life of its citizens. Now, I am very proud to be, first of all, a Blackburnian, secondly a Lancashire man, thirdly English, and fourthly a member of the United Kingdom. Those are very real things to me, of which I am proud. Outside the question of whether the Falklands war should ever have been fought, I can own, in all honesty, to standing in a pub in the markets of Birmingham, seeing a newsflash about the sinking of the Belgrano, and feeling something that I felt in the Second World War over and over again when some kind of victory was announced. It pulled at my guts in a real way, and I would be stupid to deny that it was so doing, whatever I felt about that war.

I recently watched a programme about a town in Russia, somewhere halfway between Moscow and the Polish border, celebrating the anniversary of the end of the Second World War. It was very moving to me, because it spoke very revealingly of the terrible importance to the people of that town of the experience of the Second World War and of remembering over and over again each year how the victory was won. Soon after that I was invited to a Church of England Harvest Supper. They put on a show afterwards which turned out to be exactly the same thing – about the experience of this particular parish which suffered terribly in the bombing, destroying a whole school with all their children. Although I lived as a child all through the Second World War, I had never experienced groups of people recalling it as they were doing it, so similarly in England and in Russia. So these things are real, but the question is, what claim have they on me?

For us the issue at stake is Lordship. For Christians who come under the Lordship of Christ, those identities, including that of nationality, are to be brought under His authority. Therefore while we have, from our very natures, solidarity with people in all sorts of ways, we have to find a new way of understanding this in the context of the Lordship of Christ. Industrial missioners, in South London have an interesting phrase about their work in industry and firms. They call it 'critical solidarity'. They wish to express solidarity with those in the work place, but at the same time hold the right to look at the situation under the Lordship of Christ and examine all things in terms of His justice and mercy. That is a way of expressing in their particular situation that the Lordship of Christ stands (albeit often unrecognized) over the aims and objects of the commercial and industrial complexes in which they are working.

Then there's the economic web that spreads out all over our world in both capitalist and communist systems. Once a thing is working at that scale it just runs on under its own power and momentum. Some would say that, as a case in point, 'Star Wars' is being developed because that particular military/industrial complex is actually running out of things to do. Therefore, it had to take another giant step into another area of military technology in order to keep itself occupied. The massive power behind each military/industrial complex has got to be challenged under the Lordship of Christ to reveal its own internal momentum and absolutism.

Another assumption that has to be challenged is the 'last war model' of thinking about future wars. I am always talking to people who think about nuclear war as though it is going to be like the last war. I saw an advert in *The Guardian* for survival shelters: lavishly furnished, comprehensively fitted out with full life-support survival equipment, meanwhile can be used as a luxury basement flat or wine-cellar!

There is, finally, the misunderstanding that what this world is about is a final, inevitable battle between the East and the West, between the Capitalist system and the Communist system. Every other issue has got to be subordinated to that: for instance, racism in South Africa cannot be changed because South Africa is needed as a power-base against Communism. That kind of analysis of the world situation is an absolute which twists and distorts every other thing in many people's minds. It has got to be challenged and brought under the Lordship of Christ, not to deny that there is such a polarity in the world, but to put it in proper perspective. The issue is Lordship, which challenges all these things in their reality, whether nationhood, or the power of massive economic complexes, or memory of a war which for many people was a deeply critical experience, or a false understanding of world history. These things are real, and frighteningly powerful in their reality, but where do they stand in relation to the Lordship of Christ?

'Vengeance Is Mine'

A fourth and final category of our thinking – forgiveness – is also very much at the heart of evangelical preaching and life. It confronts the absolute of revenge. If we were attacked in this country by a nuclear power, what would actually be the point of attacking them? If this country was half or totally wrecked, why retaliate? What governs that act? I suspect that it is an absolute about revenge. Yet, it clearly says in the Scriptures 'Vengeance is mine, says the Lord', and at the heart of evangelical Christianity is a belief that our task is forgiveness. We've only expressed that in our individual ways, but it has massive, public, corporate implications.

I lived in Zimbabwe (Rhodesia as it then was) for ten

years. While that country has many troubles today, there is one positive and politically unusual thing that stands out quite clearly. There was a terrible civil war in which the black people suffered a great deal, and when they took power under Robert Mugabe in 1978 there was an extraordinary act of forgiveness. The power the blacks gained was not used against the tiny white minority which had wrought terrible havoc amongst them for years. We don't know, amongst all our friends, one black family that did not suffer some death and maiming at the hands of the white-controlled Rhodesian army. But retaliation did not happen; there was forgiveness. Nations that can forgive can expect God's blessing. That is no less true under the threat of nuclear conflict.

So, in conclusion, we have these four doctrines at the heart of our belief which pertain very strongly to our work as peacemakers: the need for repentance, stewardship in preparation for the Second Coming, the Lordship of Christ and forgiveness. If we allow these to become more a part of our Christian experience, I believe we will have a particular contribution to make to the peace movement and Britain in this time.

Graham Cray

Life at St. Michael-le-Belfry (Church of England) in York is certainly not a common picture of an English parish – but nor is its vicar, Graham Cray, a traditional Anglican priest. St. Michael's is a community of Christians seeking to help renew the life of the Church in its many aspects, including worship, fellowship, mission and social concern. Graham is also a newly-elected member of the Church of England General Synod and a member of the 'Theological Support Group' for Evangelical Peacemakers – along with many other involvements.

In this chapter, which was originally a keynote address at an Evangelical Peacemakers national gathering in 1984, Graham shows how the grace and peace of God equips His people to be peacemakers in a way which is distinctive and essential.

3: 'Grace and Peace to you, from Christ Jesus'

Graham Cray

The first and most natural reaction as we consider the task before us in a nuclear age is to be daunted and fearful. The most powerful vested interests in the world are set against us. There is every reason to say, 'Lord, who are we, how do we start?'

That reaction ought to ring a few biblical bells for you. Just as it was daunting for many of God's people to respond in faith, it is also very tempting for us to be involved in peacemaking, motivated by our own fear. We fear the future, we fear what will happen, and we are fearful for our children. Those are natural fears, and in many ways, they are appropriate fears. I am in part involved in this because I *do* want there to be a world for my two little girls.

But that cannot be the root out of which our peacemaking grows. The arms race is built on fear, and peace cannot be made out of fear. Therefore, fear of the future, fear of the consequences, even fear of the bomb, cannot be the root of our peacemaking, in relation to the bomb or any other area where we need to be peacemakers. We need His transformation and His healing if we are going to be peacemakers for we cannot build peace out of fear.

But others of us, I suspect, respond with the zeal of the activist. Often the fact that one is part of a minority group feeds the sense of excitement. It is almost like the gnostic heresy in the New Testament – the people who had the real

truth that ordinary Christians were not allowed to get. There
is an energy and a sort of counterfeit power that comes out
of that and it drives one to be involved almost out of a
feeling that one is part of the elect.

It is a subtle temptation, but we need to be aware that
human activism does not bring the Kingdom of God. God
will mightily inspire energy within His servants and call
them to work beyond themselves, yes, but human activism
does not bring the Kingdom of God. There is a danger that
we might be caught up in single issue politics with a religious
veneer and have no Christian distinctiveness about our peacemaking. We would simply be in the general disarmament
movement, and we would have landed there only because
we were Christians. But that is where the Christian distinctiveness would end.

Business of the Kingdom

We are not in the business of any single issue, even of
opposing nuclear weapons. We are to be about the Kingdom
of God – and the Kingdom of God is justice and peace and
joy in the Holy Spirit. Nuclear weapons are the ultimate
blasphemy against all three of those. Therefore, the bomb is
most certainly on our agenda. But let us remember we are
not single-issue people; we are in the business of the
Kingdom, and the way we do things is to reflect the
Kingdom as well as the agenda that we take on. We will
discern the task of peacemaking and the roots of war and
violence and the arms race in a different, and in some ways
deeper, level than will the secular peace activists with whom
we will often collaborate. And collaborate we will – this is
one of these situations where they that are not against us are
with us. We need to work side by side with all who see that
this issue is central, but we will only serve them if we bring
what arises from our distinctive Christian insight.

Paul is very clear when he writes to the Corinthians, in 2
Cor. 10:3–5 'Though we live in the world, we are not
carrying on a worldly war. The weapons of our warfare are
not worldly, but have divine power to destroy strongholds.
We destroy arguments and every proud obstacle to the

knowledge of God. Make every thought captive to obey Christ.' In other words, there is going to be a totally different way of going about things in terms at least of presuppositions, that we as Christian peacemakers are going to bring.

One of my fears is that what we are doing at the moment is motivating a lot of people to get stuck into various peace groups, but very often without helping them into an understanding of what it is distinctively in the gospel of Jesus that brings them there and which will affect what they do. Paul says, 'We are not fighting against flesh and blood', including Mr. Reagan and Mrs. Thatcher and their governments, 'but principalities and powers.' He also speaks of the god of this world blinding the minds of unbelievers, to prevent them from seeing the glory of God in the face of Jesus Christ. Every aspect of the gospel and of God's glory in the face of Jesus is invisible to them, including what really makes for peace and justice. Therefore, the majority who simply do not see, and who accept policies built on fear as the only basis of defence, are not going to change anything unless the blindfold is removed.

So we are as much in the business of intercessory prayer as we are in the business of protest. We must not be pressured into thinking that the only bits that count are the bits that are seen, although those bits are important. I am not questioning any past involvements of Christians in the peace movement, but I am arguing very clearly for our need of something distinctive in the years to come.

Therefore, peacemaking must arise not only out of our Christian understanding, but primarily out of our experience of the gospel of Christ which speaks of a reversal of the world's values.

'The foolishness of God is wiser than men and the weakness of God is stronger than men and the word of the cross is folly to those who are perishing. Where is the wise man, where is the debater of this age? God has made foolish the wisdom of the world.'

Peacemaking is part of the outworking of the wisdom of God as compared with the wisdom of the world; it arises

directly out of the gospel. It is not the latest, trendy evangelical agenda that people are jumping aboard; for if it does
not arise out of the gospel, and is not seen to, it will not
last.

Grace and Peace

I want to unpack two words that, for me, summarise what
it means for peacemaking to arise out of the gospel. If I were
writing a letter to you, I would probably start off the way
Paul started off most of his letters: *Grace* to you and *Peace*
from God our Father and the Lord Jesus. *Grace* to you and
Peace. In those two words lie the roots of our ministry.

Peace, like grace, is the gift of God. 'The Lord lift up the
light of His countenance upon you and give you shalom'.
Let us remember what a big word the New Testament word
for peace is, being rooted in the Hebrew word. Peace is
God's gift and Jesus said: 'My peace I give you'. We are not
struggling to create something. We are seeking to open the
hearts of men, women, and nations so that they can receive
it. It must begin with peace with God.

Being, therefore, justified by faith, we *have* peace with
God through our Lord Jesus Christ, and that is literally the
beginning of peacemaking. Because I am reconciled to God
through the death of Jesus, that gives me a new relationship
with every other person because He *is* our peace. Each one
is called to *be* a peacemaker and to preach the gospel of the
Kingdom, which is justice and peace and joy in the Holy
Spirit. But it begins with a reconciled relationship *with* God,
which leads to the peace *of* God.

One of the dangers in this is that we have our traditional
evangelical grasp of these truths, which are often too limited
in their scope. Peace is the fruit of the Spirit. The peace of
God which passes all understanding. Peace with God. Seeing
these truths out of this limited framework causes some of us
who have caught on to the call to be peacemakers to see it
as a different kind of peace – it is another challenge to be
added. But actually the one arises out of the other. Ultimately, I cannot be a peacemaker if I am not at peace with
God. This is why the secular peace movement will struggle

so much, because there is a sense in which those who do not yet have peace, are seeking to create peace, which can only be received as God's gift. But God in His grace loves all who acknowledge what is true and honours their stand against the blasphemy of the arms race.

Peace as well as love is God's answer to fear. We are told in John 20 'that the disciples were in the upper room with the door locked for fear of the Jews'. There they were, this budding group of evangelical peacemakers, saying, 'there are so many of them and there are so few of us – lock the door and let's have a day conference!' But Jesus stands in their midst, shows to them that the future is open because He is risen. He says twice, 'Peace be with you' and the second time He breathes on them and says, 'Receive the Holy Spirit'. God's peace by the Holy Spirit, through the resurrection, is the answer to fear. Little groups who are fearful and believe they can have no real impact should think what God did with that group.

So the peacemaking that we are called to in relation to nuclear arms arises directly out of our personal encounter with God through the cross of Jesus. *Because* we have peace with God we become messengers of peace. Where we go and are received, our peace will remain.

Grace in Action

Now I want to focus on grace. I believe most evangelical Christians today do not understand the grace of God. That is quite something to say, because if there is anything we believe to have right, it would be our understanding of grace. As a boy of eight I gave my life to Jesus in a crusader class – and by the time I was 14 or 15 I could have written the most perfect essay on the doctrine of grace that could be expected of someone of my age. I am sure I would have written something about grace being an element of the nature of God and His attitudes. Of course, that is true, but that is not what Paul meant by grace. He sees God's grace in action. He is not talking about what God is *like*, he is talking about what God *does*. How many times have we sung:

'Through many dangers, toils and snares I have already come
'Twas *grace* that brought me safe thus far, and *grace* will lead me home'.

James Dunn, Professor of Divinity at Durham, writes this:

'For Paul, grace does not mean an attitude or disposition of God. It denotes rather the wholly generous act of God. Though it always, of course, carries with it the thought of God's unmerited generosity. Yes, grace is God's dealing towards us in Jesus that we do not deserve because of the death of Jesus on the cross, but it is *practical*.'

Romans 5 says: 'We have peace with God through our Lord Jesus Christ. Through Him we have obtained access to this grace in which we stand'. Paul says it is like being stuck under a waterfall of grace. You stand in the middle of it and God's grace continually comes to you. 'From His fullness have we all received grace upon grace', or, as one translation puts it 'one blessing after another'.

That is why when Paul talks about grace, he moves very quickly from the general to the specific. He sometimes uses the word *charis* (grace) and says 'By the grace given to me I bid you', or '. . . this grace was given to me to be an evangelist to the Gentiles'. He does not mean God was very merciful to forgive someone like me, who had been a persecutor of the church and turned me into an evangelist, though of course, that is true. What he means is 'I don't know why, but God called me to be an evangelist to the Gentiles, and in calling me, He empowered me with every gift and practical thing I was actually going to need to do the job. This grace was **given** to me and I was **given** the spiritual gifts I needed to fulfil this call which God will not let me escape from. You know, woe to me if I do not preach the gospel!'

If grace is to be practical in our calling to be peacemakers, we need to get the doctrine of spiritual gifts right. It is not enough to say God has called me to be a peacemaker. How, where, in what way? What is your distinctive contribution to be? Christian peacemaking is not just a matter of joining CND and going on the marches and taking the opportunities to talk about Jesus to those who ask why you are there. It is a matter of seeking God to know the specific manifestation of grace; a spiritual gift, to use James Dunn's definition, is 'any word or act which manifests the grace of God'.

Every spiritual gift involves natural ability, as well as God's activity, because God uses *you*. Even if I speak in tongues, it is my voice; the Holy Spirit does not reach down and wrench my jaws open and make the noises come out. But I do believe God gives me the words. Likewise, the spiritual gift of administration; I know people who can organise the life out of anything. Yet that gift, with the touch and call of the Spirit upon it, frees the whole body of Christ for each person to work according to gift. So each gift of the Spirit, the charisma, is a specific manifestation of *charis*. They are the powers of the coming age experienced now, right in the middle of fallen humanity.

We stand in the grace of God because we have peace with God. The Holy Spirit is just *grace* experienced. The Spirit is the member of the Godhead who is to make real to us all that Jesus *is* and has achieved for us. So grace and Spirit are again New Testament words which are closely linked together. Therefore, ask God what are the gifts of grace that He has given you to be a peacemaker and begin to order your involvement, both in this network, in your own church or wherever, according to the gifts that you discern that God has given you.

Gifts for Peacemaking

But we must note here that it is in the context of the Body of Christ that gifts are discerned. In Romans 12, 1 Cor. 12 and so on, the normal order is that people are converted to Christ, empowered by His Spirit, brought into membership of His Body, all as the beginning of their Christian experience. Then in the context of Body, one discovers what the manifestations of grace are to be, through him or her.

Now, for those who are very isolated in your churches, because others do not see, I think that this network, and especially its local meetings, has a particularly important role. As you meet together regularly, you can begin to discern spiritual gifts of peacemaking. But we will need one another for that, because our on-going conversion from fear, and all the other roots of the arms race, will only be worked out in the context of the Body of Christ. Jim Wallis of *Sojourners* magazine wrote that 'we have nothing to share with the world other than that which we are sharing with one another' and that is true. In his book called *Living Towards a Vision*, Walter Breuggemann writes this about the church:

'The little community of Shalom is free as the world is not. We are *not* victims of the powers of greed and fear and manipulation and oppression – all those powers that daily beset and beguile the world. The contrast is clear and dramatic. The big impressive world: enslaved. The little unimpressive community: free.'

We think that we have a problem being little and powerless and weak and not knowing how we are going to make any sort of impact. We owe nothing to the values of the world and because we are not attracted to them, the gods of this age have no claim upon us. We do *not* live in response to them – Hallelujah!

If the result of our peacemaking and of all our other witness for Christ is to lead people to faith in the power of God, rather than in our arguments, something very deep has to happen in us. The power of God, the grace of God, as Paul teaches about it, is *always* in the context of human weakness, because as far as the world is concerned, the gospel is weakness. But the weakness of God is stronger than human strength and, therefore, Paul will say that he will gladly boast about the things that show his weakness that the power of Christ may rest upon him. 'My *grace* is sufficient for you – my *power* is made perfect in weakness.' Therefore, *grace* is not to *replace* weakness. *Grace* is to be present in the context of weakness so that people may experience the power of God.

I think we have problems with both ends of that. We do

not like being weak, and we are also afraid of the power of
God. Paul says an amazing thing in 1 Cor. 13:4 – 'Jesus was
crucified in weakness; he lives by the power of God for we
are weak in Him'.

Isn't that extraordinary? You would not expect it; you
would expect we are *strong* in Him. 'Be strong in the Lord
and the strength of His might' and so on. That is obviously
true, but in this context Paul says: 'We are *weak* in Him' –
and when I am weak I am strong. When I recognize my
inability and my weakness that I cannot, with all my zeal,
bring peace to this world, that my efforts, however deeply
I have understood the gospel in my head, cannot bring peace
by itself.

The first call of peacemakers is to understand our total
powerlessness to be peacemakers. 'My grace is sufficient for
you, my power is made perfect in weakness.' Paul never
ever boasted of his gifts. He said, 'I won't dare to speak
except of what Christ has done through me. And the things
I will boast about are the things that show me to be weak,
to myself and to other people.'

I think we need three things for that to happen. I believe
we need to ask God to break each one of us. You can only
be a peacemaker if you are willing to be defenceless. There
is so much in me that springs to my own defence; but while
I cling to my strength, I grieve and resist and quench the
Spirit of God and try to live apart from God's grace. Most
of us trust our ability when we feel capable and the grace of
God when we feel stuck. God has got to make us the sort
of people who trust His grace in everything, who will then
give all that we are to cooperate with Him. The grace of
God bringing the power of God, through people like you
and me, is the only thing that will bring peace. That is where
our abilities come in.

I am staggered by the second letter to the Corinthians.
Paul wrote it to re-establish his authority among the believers
after some more charismatic people had come along and
claimed to be apostles.

'We do not want you to be ignorant, brethren, of the
afflictions we experienced in Asia. We were so utterly,

unbearably crushed, we despaired of life itself. We felt we had received the sentence of death, but that was to make us rely not on ourselves, but on God who raises the dead. He delivered us from so deadly a peril. He *will* deliver us. On Him we set our hope – He will deliver us again. *You* must help us by prayer'.

To get his authority back, he writes a letter and tells of his utter despair in life. Totally, unbearably crushed, but he simply said 'You have got to help us by praying for us – we cannot make it without your prayers.'

Communities of the Tender Hearted

If we are serious about peacemaking, God will bring us to some similar experience. It might be through circumstances, it might be through what is going on within us, that we'll come to that time when we can no longer rely on ourselves. At that point, the grace of God will be able to break through. God only breaks hearts to heal them, that we may be tender-hearted. But He calls us to be weak, He calls us to be broken, He calls us to be vulnerable, and out of that he builds a community of the tender-hearted who live vulnerable and defenceless lives with one another which then become demonstrations of His peace – communities ruled by the peace of Christ.

We need demonstrations of the alternative as well as protests against what we have got at the present, and only if we let God do some deep things in us is that going to happen. I believe we need to look to the time when the stream within charismatic renewal, which is open to God's signs and wonders, and the stream of evangelicalism that is deeply committed to the ministry of peace, actually flow together.

The Lord Jesus healed the ear of the servant of those who came to arrest Him, and there was, if you like, a 'peace-making sign and wonder' right in the middle of the betrayal. Why don't we see some policemen healed on demonstrations? I'd like to see the power of God doing things that touch lives of those who, because of their official role in

society, such as the armed forces of the police, find themselves touched by the grace of God right in the middle of
confronting people like us. We have to be open to far more
than just enemy-loving and non-violence; we need to be the
means with which the grace of God may minister the power
of God to those who find themselves opposing us.

We will be peacemakers to the extent to which we allow
God to forge those things in us, so that we come to rely
on them and on Him, and not on ourselves. Unless our
peacemaking arises out of that experience, we will not be
evangelical peacemakers.

J. Andrew Kirk

If there is anyone among British evangelicals who is teaching us how to think biblically and radically, Andrew Kirk is certainly foremost among them. Andrew brings not only a thorough and scholarly approach to his teaching and writing ministry, he also brings the perspectives gained from many years of living in the two-thirds world. After teaching theology in Argentina for CMS. (Church Missionary Society), he returned to his native England and is now theologian missioner for CMS. and associate director of the London Institute for Contemporary Christianity. He has written *Liberation Theology: An Evangelical Perspective*, *Theology Encounters Revolution*, and most recently *A New World Coming*.

For many people, a consideration of the issues surrounding nuclear weapons brings with it a question about the state. What is a Christian's proper relationship to the government under which they live? As Andrew shows in the following chapter, these issues are not, of course, different in a nuclear age, but certainly more pressing.

4: A Biblical View of the Nuclear State

J. Andrew Kirk

The threat of nuclear war has concentrated afresh the minds of both political analysts and ordinary people on the place of the nation-state in the modern world.

The ability of a few governments to unleash an awesome, destructive force against other territories discloses the height to which the military might of some nations has ascended. Coupled with this, there has been an increasing tendency on the part of these same nations to ridicule, suffocate, or bludgeon dissent in the interest of 'security'.

Such unparalleled power in the hands of a relatively small group of people, claiming to represent the whole populous, though only accountable to them in general terms every four of five years, has led Christians in recent years to consider deeply their responsibility within the state. No longer does it seem possible just to acquiesce in the continuing political life of a nation, for the stakes are far too high.

The existence of massive amounts of nuclear warheads, ready to launch when the computers signal, 'strike', are seriously challenging traditional notions of citizenship. This short essay will attempt to present some of the biblical evidence that bears on the subject of Christian witness to the state. At the end I will attempt to draw some specific conclusions that may help those who confess Jesus Christ as Lord and God to decide what their own attitudes to the issue of nuclear war should be.

There are two contexts in which, I believe, the relationship between church and state should be viewed. One, obviously, is God's purposes in creation and redemption in a wide sense, covering both the nature and mission of the church and the functions of the state. The other context is the actual situation of church and state in any particular concrete reality. The first of these touches on the ideal relationship between church and state; the second deals with a reality probably very far removed from the ideal.

Approaching the Bible

God's purposes have to be read out of the text of Scripture. This is not a totally straightforward exercise. We must, therefore, give some account of the method of approaching Scripture which we believe is right.

For the purposes of this study, let me suggest two complementary approaches to Scripture. One is the exegetical, which proceeds by way of an inductive analysis of specific texts, allowing us to see the rich diversity of Scripture. This method shows how God's word is given in specific contexts and for specific purposes. We have to interpret the Scriptures against that background and in that light. Secondly, there is a thematic approach, which seeks to compare texts and discover underlying historical developments and theological consistency. This method focuses on the unity of Scripture.

The first task involves the gathering of material. What portions of Scripture are relevant to the debate? By what criteria do we choose? How do we relate the passages and themes together? Christians answer these questions in different ways. The fact of giving unequal weight to the same passages, or relating the Old and New Testaments differently, creates the diversity. One group of Christians cannot necessarily claim a greater biblical integrity than another; rather, the approach and questions asked are different.

So we cannot avoid the hermeneutical questions, for the concepts and experiences of both church and state are diverse. Our own partial understanding and perspective will influence the amount of weight we give to different strands of the biblical evidence. For example, the Roman Catholic and Anabaptist understandings of the church have been shaped by different experiences and interpretations of historical events. These have led to the acceptance and reverencing of different traditions, which in turn tend to be justified by a particular reading of the text.

A similar problem arises when we consider such questions as authority and participation in public life, the accountability of power and the question of what constitutes the will of the people.

Once having adopted a position it is difficult to move. Perhaps in the interests of greater agreement among Christians, we should ask what makes people move their positions. What convinces them that their convictions may not have been correct, or at least not the whole truth?

Bridging the gaps between divergent scriptural interpretations cannot be achieved from a detached vantage point. We are each a product of a specific social and cultural history, geographically located. This immersion greatly influences us and accounts often for the intense emotion which is generated about contemporary matters of justice, peace, and freedom in society. We are conditioned by our social situation and our church affliation, though never determined in a mechanistic sense.

God's Spirit, however, enables individuals and groups to listen to God's Word and to one another, challenging and reformulating opinions carried from the past. This fact is powerful evidence of the efficacy of the Gospel. Listening is a prerequisite for discovering what the Lord requires in specific circumstances.

Church and State in the Old Testament

An overview of the entire Bible will begin to point to the general themes and situations which need to be included in any discussion of church and state.

For the sake of convenience I will divide the Old Testament into three parts:

- pre-history, comprehending the first eleven chapters of

Genesis (the title is not intended as a comment on its historical worth);
- 'covenantal history', comprehending the period from Abraham to the restoration of Israel from exile: it focuses on God's dealing with Israel in the context of the nations;
- 'prophetic history', referring to passages which trace the future direction of God's sovereign rule over all things and all people.

Let us then try to set both Church and state into this framework. The Church does not exactly exist in the period of 'prehistory'; rather it begins with the people of Abraham and includes (through the marriages of Isaac and Jacob and possibly others) both the kindred left in Ur and those who went with Abraham to Canaan.

From the beginning it has a double identity. It is both a pilgrim people and a nation (Gen. 12:1–2). The church in the Old Testament is the people of God related to Abraham. It has, therefore, an inescapable ethnic identity. In Egypt they were both the people of Israel as well as the Hebrews who did not integrate into national life (Ex. 1:9–10). At this stage, they were not yet a nation, but an immigrant community.

They became a nation when they were liberated from slavery and were given the space and freedom to organise themselves according to God's specifications. For this to happen they needed to be free both from external threats (other people) and internal threats (idolatry).

Israel, Both Church and Nation

The church in the Old Testament is then a nation with a geographical boundary, institutions such as elders, and laws to regulate its life. But it is also a people, an assembly of clans, tribes, and families, convoked by God, bound to him by a solemn covenant and existing for a specific purpose. It is a *priestly* kingdom and a *holy* nation. It has a life to live, both as a *nation* among the other nations and as a *people* which is to be God's agent to bring light and blessing to the whole world.

As a nation, Israel has to order its social affairs to make daily living a possibility. It exists as any other nation to fulfil the so-called creation and cultural mandates. It also exists within a reality marked by the effects of sin – idolatry, injustice, violence. But as a pilgrim people it looks to the fulfilment of God's redemptive purposes. It exists in this sense not only *among* the nations, but *for* the nations. It is the one for the many. Therefore its daily living also has to be an exercise in liberation. As the law makes abundantly clear, it is to live the justice, shalom, and freedom of the rule of Yahweh. Hence the prophetic visions of the future are also challenges to return to the terms of the covenant from which Israel has departed. By desiring to be as the other nations, they have become a people which has turned its back on liberation, content to live on a level of normal sinful relationships (such as allowing power and wealth to concentrate in only a few hands).

The church in the Old Testament, then, is an assembly of people related to Abraham by birth, and to God by both an act of liberation and a solemn covenant based on God's law of liberty (Ex. 24:7–8, Jas. 2.12). There was, so to speak, no separation of church and state. Israel was to be a society modelled after the character of God, the One who requires that every aspect of life should reflect the twin principles of *mishpat* (justice) and *hesed* (mercy) (Mic. 6:8, Ps. 85:10–13).

Israel's relationship to Yahweh was not one simply of right ethical conduct in terms of social life and personal relationships. As a people they were to trust Yahweh for everything that brought abundant life and joy, good produce from land and health. This trust was to extend to Israel as a nation. They were to look also to Yahweh for peace from external enemies. Yahweh, as in Egypt and in the desert wanderings, would protect his people from aggression. Of course, security was intimately related to obedience to Yahweh's standard of right living. The territorial integrity of Israel was never inviolate, independent of whether Israel kept the terms of the covenant or not.

Different From Other Nations

Israel was set among the nations. She was part of an historical reality of international power politics. The nations were characterised by the fruit of their idolatry, arrogant violence, corruption and exploitation. Religion, as practised by the nations, was often a legitimation of injustice and oppression.

Israel, however, was called to be something entirely different. It was, in political and military terms, insignificant (Deut. 7:7). It was given strict instructions not to be as the other nations (Deut. 17). The ruler of Israel was to be one among equals. He was to be taken from among his brethren. He was not to have a large standing army, nor enter into military alliances, nor accumulate wealth for himself. Indeed, kingship was seen as a concession to Israel's weakness (I Sam. 8), not part of the deal of a holy nation. The centralisation of power, authority, and wealth are related to a rejection of Yahweh (I Sam. 10:17–19), the direct consequence of refusing to rely solely on him for peace and prosperity.

The nations, however, were not outside of God's concern for justice and mercy. They figure in the period of prehistory, the generations of the sons of Noah for example (Gen. 10:5, 20, 31–32), and they are part of God's ultimate redemptive purpose (Is. 2:3–4, 45:14, 55:5, 66:18–21; Zech. 8:20–23; Rev. 22:2). Meanwhile the nations are expected to live according to the law written into the nature of every human being, what Amos calls the 'covenant of brotherhood' (Amos 1:9). Substantial portions of the prophetic writings are given over to oracles upon the nations. God holds every nation morally accountable. The standard of judgment may not be the explicit demands of the Decalogue and the Book of the Covenant, but the implicit, innate sense of justice which every human being possesses, manifested both in the condemnation of others (Rom. 2:1–2) and in righteous acts (Rom. 2:6–10).

The main difference between Israel and the nations is one of time sequence in God's plan. God's revelation of himself, his requirements, and his provision of salvation, are given first to Israel. Israel has been elected to be a light to the nations, to bring justice to the ends of the earth. This it will do after a probationary period when it had itself drunk deeply from the wells of God's law.

This time lag between Israel and the rest of the nations explains the change of relationships between them prior to, during, and since the settlement of the promised land. Whereas Israel was used as an instrument to judge the wickedness and idolatry of the nations at the time of occupation, later the roles were reversed: and nations were sent to judge Israel for its faithlessness and disobedience. There is no difference of kind in God's dealings with all his creation. Israel was never favoured for its own sake, nor is any other nation. God shows no partiality. Justice (*mishpat*) and grace (*hesed*) have always been the way God works.

Church and State in the New Testament

The New Testament might be divided in the following way:

a) Jesus and the Kingdom among the Jews
b) Jesus and the Kingdom from the crucifixion to Pentecost
c) Jesus and the Kingdom among Jewish believers
d) Jesus and the Kingdom in the Church of the Gentile Mission
e) Jesus and the consummation of the Kingdom.

The purpose of these divisions and those of the Old Testament is to offer a general historical framework for the discussion of each instance of church and state.

One of the necessities of the debate is to hold fast to the immensely wide vision of Scripture concerning God's plan for the universe. Our political life, though experienced with great intensity and seriousness, is but a pinprick on the vast scan of God's history.

When we come to the New Testament the relationship between church and state clearly changes. Many of our difficulties stem from the fact that interpreters of the Scripture do not altogether concur about the nature of the change. Most would agree, however, that two major aspects of God's purposes come into closer focus:

a) The coming of the Messiah brings a crisis, a judgment, into the heart of the Israelite people/nation. The call to discipleship and faith provokes a division among the populous. From now on two communities exist side by side. The reason for the division is given theological consideration by Paul in Romans 9–11. He concludes that the reality is not new but brought into sharp relief by the presence of the Christ. God has always based his relationship with his people on his calling and not on ethnic identity. Therefore his people are bound to him by faith and obedience and not by fulfilling the ritual and cultural requirements of the nation: the works of the law. It was the choice between the two which brought a separation between Jew and Jew (Luke 17:33–35). Paul then develops his theological explanation of what has happened around the theme of the remnant (Rom. 2:28–29, 4:13–17, 9:6–8).

b) God's people are no longer identified with one nation. Though the incorporation of Greeks, Barbarians and Scythians into the people of God was hard for the early Christian Jews to approve, the time came when the apostolic leadership of the new community of the Messiah accepted that this was the fulfilment of God's pre-ordained plan. According to the promise to Abraham, the logic of election and grace, and the prophetic testimony to the Day of the Lord, all the peoples are included in God's provision of salvation. It is this fact above all others which poses the dilemma concerning the church's relationship to the state.

Jesus and the Kingdom

The story and message of the New Testament centres on Jesus and the Kingdom. Both God's special people and the state in different ways derive their meaning and functions from these two events.

Jesus, in his public ministry, declared that the Kingdom had broken into the daily reality of people and nations and showed that its power was operative in nature, in personal relationships, and in religious and political life.

Jesus' call to discipleship, 'Follow me', is therefore a call to seek first the Kingdom and its justice, to enter that Kingdom and to take its yoke upon one. God's people are invited and challenged to orientate their whole lives round his Kingdom. The church, therefore, finds its identity as the sign and first-fruits of the Kingdom.

The One who issues the call, however, is not like the Scribes and Pharisees. He is greater than Solomon and Jonah. The post-resurrection confession, 'My Lord and my God' (Jn. 20:28) is an irreplaceable foundation of New Testament belief. Jesus of Nazareth *is* King of the Jews, and of the Romans as well (Jn. 19:11).

Authority in the public life of communities is therefore an exercise of power which is relative, derived and accountable. In the political and religious drama preceding the crucifixion, the Jews, moved by the dynamic of the false accusations of blasphemy which they laid against Jesus, were forced themselves to utter the supreme blasphemy, 'We have no King but Caesar' (John 19:15).

Lords and deities of all kinds are subjected to the one supreme Lord over all (I Cor. 8:5, 6). Within this relationship, however, civil authorities have divinely-granted functions and responsibilities. This seemed to be the point Paul wanted to convey in the famous and much-disputed passage Romans 13:1–7.

The Governing Authorities

According to the immediate context, Romans 12:17–21, the Christians in Rome were tempted to take the law into their own hands and apply the principle of retribution against their persecutors (Rom. 12:14, 19). This, deriving perhaps from a misguided interpretation of freedom in Christ, was not permitted to them in God's arrangement of human life.

Paul goes on to say that the governing authorities were to repay evil with evil by bringing punishment on the wrongdoer. Presumably in this case the wrongdoing was committed both by some who were persecuting Christians and by some Christians who retaliated in kind.

The state's responsibility, then, is to maintain harmony and peace within a society always likely to break apart into open factions. More than that, it is to promote harmony by rewarding good. Paul has in mind here the state faithfully fulfilling its God-appointed tasks. Its work is defined and circumscribed by the good, that is to say the absolute justice required by God, not by its own laws. When Paul says (v.1) 'For there is not an authority except by God', he is saying more than that God has established actual particular governing bodies. He implies that no authority either establishes or authenticates itself. It does not give power to itself nor, by deduction, does it receive power from the people.

God's sovereign authority over all powers means that governments are God's servants (Paul uses the words *diakonoi* and *leitonergoi* to express their responsibility to serve) in so far as they carefully attend to these matters of administering justice and being the agent for the punishment of evil. They cease, however, to offer God service and worship as soon as they compromise over justice and injustice.

God's sovereignty also requires Christians to *submit* to the reality of authority (*hupotassein*); they are not, however, necessarily to obey (*hupakonein*) every injunction of every individual state.

In commenting on Christ's famous phrase concerning the payment of tax, 'Render to Caesar what is Caesar's and to God what is God's', Miranda in his book *Communism and the Bible* links it to the statement 'You cannot serve both God and money.' In this latter verse it is likely that the original Aramaic verb used was *abad* which means divine service or worship. Miranda argues that when Jesus was shown the coin with the Emperor's head on it he says, 'Give back' [*apodidonai*—not just 'give' but 'give back'] to Caesar what belongs to him [that is to say, the money which is served in the place of God] and to God what belongs to Him.' In other words, the state only has a limited function to receive taxes in order to carry on its legitimate work (Rom. 13:7). We are to submit to it in this sense, but never to serve it, for divine service (*abad, leitovergia*) belongs only to God.

The State and Idolatry

It is not surprising that there is a strong biblical tradition which sets the state in the context of idolatry and even demonology (which we find in Daniel and Revelation in particular). The state may find it impossible to distinguish between submission and service. It is constantly tempted to turn itself into an autonomous object of reverence, and to demand an allegiance which goes beyond its legitimate right. Moreover, failing to recognise and acknowledge its own subordinate, derived and secular authority, it gradually ascribes to itself a religious value, a personalised being to be subjected to. The picture of Rome in the Book of Revelation is one, along with the Old Testament descriptions of Egypt, Assyria, and Babylon.

The inevitable outcome of the state's proud self-assertion will be a conflict with the church. Most states of the ancient world encouraged a distinction between public religion, a formality by which one could pay one's respects to the divine nature of the King or Emperor, and private belief, a matter of individual choice and of indifference to the state. Most modern states maintain the tradition in the form either of a Volks Religion, in which religion ministers to the symbols of state authority, or of a totally secular government in which religion is not allowed to interfere with the practice of power.

The early church could not make the distinction between public and private. In the public realm the demand is for a non-religious state in which the church has no particular privileged place, held religiously accountable to the one Lord of all. The ideal for the state to be God's instrument of his justice and the reality of its easy slide into idolatry, accounts for the church's sporadic resistance to all the state's absolutist claims for itself or for any of its policies. This resistance by the church when circumstances demand, is made possible only when it is true to God's complete revelation; it may be considered part of the church's submission, to the end that the state may better reflect what God constituted.

The church inevitably has as one of its functions that of being a catalyst (in totalitarian societies, often the only one) for criticism whenever the state abandons its God-given role. This criticism is to be balanced by praying for all authorities and seeking the welfare, not the destruction, of society. The church can fulfil this dual calling because it is no longer a nation, but a group called out to be followers of Jesus, because it is a people made up of many nationalities and because it bears witness to the perfection of a new order of life which God is creating.

The Christian's Responsibility to the State

All the modern nuclear states subscribe to the ideal of a secularised society. This means that government policies are largely created without serious consideration of the absolute values of human dignity and social justice. Moreover, they would be loath to accept the Christian view that both the easy corruption of power and the strong tendency to rationalise all political decisions flow from a perverted human nature which distorts the whole of life. In other words, they recognise neither God nor evil (except, perhaps, as it exists among the 'enemy').

A Christian however begins to consider the question of the use of state power from the assumption that it is accountable to the one God who has instituted it. He or she is likely therefore to feel intensely unhappy with the state's general inability to recognise that there are truths which go beyond the apparent dimensions of *realpolitik*.

It is in the light of an utterly realistic view of the actual practice of political life that a Christian may be said to have both a passive and active obligation towards civil authority: passive in the sense of not transgressing laws duly established by the bodies with authority to pass them, active in witnessing to and promoting the justice and peace of the Kingdom. In both cases the point of reference will be the living God and not the civil powers themselves. We will submit because our consciences are attuned to the ways of God. Submission may entail either obedience or disobedience.

In the realm of warfare and peacemaking the following conclusions seem to me to flow from our studies (I realise that other people may derive other opinions from the same arguments):

● A nation is a useful, identifiable entity which represents a particular geographical locality in which justice may be done and be seen to be done. No nation, made up today of many different peoples (peoples is the biblical category rather than nation), is wholly inviolate. It is the recipient of God's common grace and is under his judgment. It may disappear, as did five-sixths of Israel. No nation is a law to itself. It is beholden to treat other nations with respect and integrity. It is doubtful whether the modern and common idea of national sovereignty has much foundation in God's purposes for the nations; it may be little more than tribalism or communalism.

● No nation has an absolute right to defend itself.* The situation may arise, as in the case of Judah in Jeremiah's time, when it should lay aside its arms, abandon its treaties with Egypt and Syria, and allow itself to be invaded. A Christian's response to a government imposed from outside is the same as that to an elected government: submission which, depending on the policies adopted, may mean obedience or disobedience.

● In other circumstances a nation may defend itself from an aggressor. However, the defence is not on the basis of sovereignty, but on the basis that the society being attacked is more an approximation to the justice and peace of the Kingdom than that of the aggressor.

● God's people belong to two different groups in society. They belong to all the other members of Christ's body. This loyalty is paramount, for the Body of Christ is already a part of the Age to Come (Heb. 6:4–5). It represents God's future, the promised new order marked by resurrection and transfiguration. But they also belong to the people into which they were born. They are part of a natural family, not all of which will belong to God's family, and to which

---

* Many Christians believe that the disproportionate destruction unleashed in a nuclear exchange negates the usual argument for limited retaliation against an aggressor, namely legitimate self-defence. In Christian ethical thinking, the ends do not automatically justify the means. A nuclear holocaust could never be the lesser of two evils.

they also have obligations. These two belongings may conflict and they will have to be balanced according to different situations. Thus the church may not always and invariably possess the mind of Christ in a situation of conflict between nations. Christian people on both sides of a rift need to listen carefully to their brethren on the other side, and critically to the voice of the government on their own.

Alan Kreider

If you are a Christian, living in Britain, and concerned about nuclear weapons, it is quite likely that at some point you have come across our next author. Alan Kreider has for many years, been working to raise issues of peace and war among evangelicals as issues of faith. Whilst being involved in this, he has also served as an elder of the London Mennonite Fellowship, a congregation representing the historic peace church, founded during the 'radical reformation'.

It is appropriate that Alan should offer us a meditation on the prophet Ezekiel as he has so often called British evangelicals to return to the Scriptures and to be truly faithful to them. The questions he poses about the nature of the prophetic calling, and the discernment of true from false prophecy, confronts us all with the need to approach God in humility as well as in confidence.

5: Watching or Whitewashing?

Alan Kreider

What is God saying about the crises of our time? What is his message to us about the nuclear bomb?

Unfortunately, the Bible does not say anything directly about the bomb. And although many churchpersons and theologians agree that the Bible contains an eloquent *indirect* word for our time, they disagree as to what the word is. 'Our God comes, he does not keep silence,' thundered an ancient Hebrew poet (Ps 50:3). What is he really saying? How can we hear him above the fads and fears of our time?

One way to hear God today is to find situations in the past in which he was speaking and listen to those. Parallels between events in biblical history and those in our own time can never be precise. But even so, they may be close enough to be helpful to discriminate between God's competing spokespersons today and thereby to discern what God is saying to *us*.

Let us allow ourselves to be transported 2600 years into history to listen to the experience of Ezekiel. There were, to be sure, no nuclear bombs then. But perhaps there are other parallels which will help us to unclutter our minds and to listen to God afresh. After all, the Bible claims that God was speaking to that situation. Does the word that he was trying to communicate then help us to hear his word to us?

The Setting

Ezekiel was a refugee. In 597 BC he, along with other aristocratic Jerusalemites, had been deported to the country-side not far from the enemy capital, Babylon. His pain of dislocation was intensified by his inability to carry on his professional life. For Ezekiel was a Jewish priest, far from the temple in which he had ministered. It was not, however, in the temple that Ezekiel first 'saw visions of God'. It was under foreign skies, among exiles, by the river Chebar, that 'the heavens were opened' and Ezekiel the priest became a prophet (Ez 1:1).

Life in Babylon was not easy for Ezekiel. Although 500 miles from Jerusalem, he obviously stayed well informed – probably by letter – of the distressing developments among the Jews who had been allowed to remain behind. In these events what was Yahweh doing? A man of intense spiritual sensitivity, Ezekiel wrestled with this question in vivid and terrifying visions.

In one of these visions, Yahweh told Ezekiel that these spiritual experiences were not for his own private delec-tation. 'Son of man,' Yahweh addressed him, 'I have made you a *watchman* for the house of Israel; whenever you hear a word from my mouth, you shall give them warning from me' (Ez 3:17). To be a watchman was to be responsible – responsibile to communicate to people a message from God which would enable them to turn around. If he failed in this, God would hold him accountable for their fate.

But communicating God's warning to the Israelites was difficult. This was not simply because Ezekiel could convey his messages only by letter. More seriously, it was because Ezekiel faced competition from other prophets.

Ezekiel could thunder the direst of threats: 'You have feared the sword, and I will bring the sword upon you, says Yahweh God. And I will bring . . . you into the hands of foreigners, and execute judgements upon you; . . . for you have not walked in my statutes' (Ez 11:8–12). But in Jeru-salem there were authoritative religious figures giving a different message. Prophets like Hananiah also spoke in the name of Yahweh: 'I have broken the yoke of the king of

Babylon. Within two years I will bring back to this place
. . . all the exiles' (Jer 28:2–4). And there were many Hanan-
iahs. To whom should the Jerusalemites listen: Ezekiel, the
isolated exile of fevered imagination whose message required
repentance? or the reassuring prophets of the Jerusalem
Establishment?

Sooner or later Ezekiel would have to address this question
by facing his competitors head-on. A word of Yahweh
enabled him to do so with integrity: 'Son of man, prophesy
against the prophets of Israel' (Ez 13:2). In the message which
followed, Yahweh ushered Ezekiel into the middle of the
arena in which for centuries the prophets – genuine and
bogus – had been contending. There was now a greater
urgency than ever before: Jerusalem, the last vestige of independent Israelite political life, would within a decade be
trampled under the Babylonian boot and destroyed – unless
the people repented. But this urgency was the only novel
element in the message to Ezekiel. For centuries, in both
Israel and Judah, Yahweh's case against the prophets had
remained constant.

They Lie and Do Not Listen

What were his grievances? There were three, in the
expression of which Ezekiel was simply the latest in a long
tradition of Yahweh's messengers. First of all, Yahweh
accused the respectable prophets of lying. 'They have spoken
falsehood and divined a lie' (Ez 13:6). By assuring the inhabitants of Jerusalem that they would be secure without
repenting, the prophets were saying something that simply
wasn't true. In their moral confusion, they may not have
recognized this; apparently they genuinely expected Yahweh
to carry out what they said (13:6). But Yahweh would not
do it. Their vision was 'delusive.' Despite their excellent
connections and impressive credentials, their message was
unreal, unrealistic.

Ezekiel was not told *why* his prophetic antagonists were
addicted to the lie. Indirectly, perhaps, he charged them with
economic self-interest. The 'foxes among the ruins' to which
he likens them were primarily concerned with their own

dens and with scavenging for their own carrion. But Ezekiel was not as forthright as Micah, who charged that the court prophets 'cry "Shalom" when they have something to eat' (Mic 3:5; see also Jer 6:13).

Nor in this passage did Ezekiel develop his analysis of the official prophets on the basis of political pressure or social conditioning. Micaiah had been told: 'Behold, the words of the prophets with one accord are favourable to the king; let your word be like the word of one of them, and speak favourably' (1 Kings 22:13) – or else! And even without overt pressure, what other than an optimism which blesses the status quo could one expect to come from a court? Ezekiel, however, simply registers the fact of the prophets' falsehood – and of Yahweh's outrage: 'My hand will be against the prophets who see delusive visions and who give lying divinations.' By Yahweh's decree, it is *they* who shall become exiled, not just from Jerusalem but from Yahweh's people: 'they shall not be in the council of my people . . . and you shall know that I am Yahweh God' (Ez 13:9).

Second, Yahweh accused the Establishment prophets of failing in the fundamental task of the prophet – listening to Yahweh. They use the right religious formulas – 'Hear the word of Yahweh' – but they themselves have not heard it. But since prophecy is their metier and their public duties require them to say something, they 'prophesy out of their own minds' (Ez 13:2). Unlike Ezekiel, they are spiritually insensitive. Having 'seen nothing', they have no choice but to 'follow their own spirit' (13:3).

How unlike Micah they are! 'As for me, I am filled with power, with the Spirit of Yahweh, with justice and might, to declare to Jacob his transgression and to Israel his sin' (Mic 3:8). If only they, like Jeremiah, had 'stood in the council of Yahweh to perceive and to hear his word' (Jer 23:18). Lacking this attentiveness, they have no choice but to give expression to their own hopes and self-interest. Small wonder that Yahweh, in whose name they speak, is against them.

Popularised Prophecy

Yahweh's third accusation is a product of the first two: the prophets were telling the people what they wanted to hear. What could any good Jew desire more than *shalom*? This radiant expression of Yahweh's all-embracing concern for human welfare, of his intertwining of everything that made for wholeness, was to the Jewish mind the most exalted expression of earthly happiness. In daily life, *shalom* as a greeting graced their social interchanges. And it was not accidental that the centre of their national religion was named Jerusalem – foundation of *shalom*. Health, right relationships, justice, physical safety, good harvests, prosperity, the presence of Yahweh – all these were encapsulated in this mighty but brief word.

The Jerusalemites of Ezekiel's day knew that they were threatened. Compared to the economic and military muscle of Babylon, their tiny kingdom was puny. Already they had been forced to concede treasure and hostages to the Babylonian king Nebuchadrezzar. And yet, despite these geopolitical realities, Yahweh promises them *shalom*. The prophets say so! How encouraging it is to hear what you want to hear from a supposedly unimpeachable source.

But it is precisely the encouragement of this wishful thinking, which confirmed people in their customary ways and prevented them from repenting, which was the heart of Yahweh's complaint against the prophets. 'They have misled my people,' he lamented through Ezekiel. They have said ' "*shalom*" ', when there is no shalom' (Ez 13:10; cf Jer 6:14; 8:11). The people, in their construction of false securities, have *built a wall*.

In his attack upon the prophets, Ezekiel does not tell us what the wall was, but in chapter 17 he gives us a clue. Zedekiah, king of Judah, has rebelled against the Babylonians who are Yahweh's instruments of judgement 'by sending ambassadors to Egypt, that they might give him horses and a large army' (17:15). But trusting in alliances and weaponry would fail: 'Pharaoh with his mighty army and great company will not help him in time of war' (17:17). The wall thus was human artefacts and arrangements in which people put their trust. The false prophets, according to Jeremiah, made the people 'trust in a lie' (Jer 28:15). What Zedekiah, with the encouragement of the court prophets, was doing was not new. Listen to Isaiah: 'Woe to those who go down to Egypt for help [alliances] and rely on horses, and trust in chariots [state-of-the-art military hardware]' (Is 31:1; cf 2 Chron 16:7). The delusory things in which people trust could also include an unjust economic order: 'Because you . . . trust in oppression and perverseness, and rely on them, therefore this iniquity shall be to you like a break in a high wall, bulging out, and about to collapse, whose crash comes suddenly' (Is 30:12–13).

Above all, the wall in which the prophets and people of Jerusalem trusted was their religiosity. While the temple sacrifices carry on, while the prophets continue to pronounce 'says Yahweh,' the people 'have taken their idols into their hearts' (Ez 14:3). They have assumed that Yahweh is tolerant, that they can both have his blessing and live by the standards of other gods. After all, they continue to maintain the temple cult: 'This is the temple of Yahweh, the temple of Yahweh, the temple of Yahweh' (Jer 7:4).

Whitewashing Sin

The wall, Ezekiel knew full well, was tottering. Cobbled together of shoddy military, economic and religious materials, it had no structural strength. And what were the Establishment prophets doing? Rather than examining the wall and acknowledging its battered slate, rather than taking their place in its breaches (Ez 13:5), rather than calling the people to trust in Yahweh instead of in these false securities, they were *whitewashing* the wall. How it gleams in the gloss of prophetic approval! Surrounded by a wall of *shalom*, the state of Judah will be secure.

But it won't be. Ezekiel, not the court prophets, is the realist. For he had heard Yahweh's voice: 'Say to those who daub [the wall] with whitewash that it will fall!' Yahweh himself would demolish it: 'I will make a stormy wind break out in my wrath; and there shall be a deluge of rain in my anger, and great hailstones in wrath to destroy it' (Ez

13:11–13). Hailstones – terrifying, bombarding, atomizing, in Jewish history indicating the direct military intervention of Yahweh (Josh 10:11; Job 38:23; Is 30:30): these Yahweh would direct at his people's false securities. When that happens, 'they will seek *shalom*, but there shall be none' (Ez 7:25).

Amidst the wreckage, the prophets' superficial optimism will be exposed. Babylonian battering rams will demonstrate the falsity of their flattery. Under attack, the whitewashed wall's foundations will be laid bare. And in the general carnage, the prophets themselves will die. Then, at last but too late, they will have a true perspective: 'you shall know that I am Yahweh' (Ez 13:14). How furious Yahweh was at the watchmen turned whitewashers who spoke in his name, who saw visions of *shalom* when there was no shalom.

Yet this doesn't need to happen, says Ezekiel. He must have sensed that there was very little time, but there was *enough time*. There was time for the Jerusalemites to ignore the soothing words of their prophets and to repent. 'Get yourselves a new heart and a new spirit! Why will you die, O house of Israel? For I have no pleasure in the death of anyone, says Yahweh God; so turn, and live' (Ez 18:31–32).

The people didn't turn, and the time ran out. In 586 BC, seven years after Ezekiel's first visions, Yahweh brought upon the Jewish people 'the fruit of their devices' (Jer 6:19). The Babylonian war machine pulverized the pearl of Jewish civilization, Jerusalem. The temple was devastated; and all those, including their prophets, who were not killed in the sacking of the city were deported to die – alongside Ezekiel – by the waters of Babylon. The city's lack of *shalom*, which a true prophet had detected beneath the coat of whitewash, was now evident to all.

There is something perennial in the accusations which Ezekiel brought against the prophets of his time. Jesus, for example, speaking six hundred years after Ezekiel, used similar language in his debates with the religious leaders of his day. Once again, a temple had been built, the centre of sacrifice and spiritual respectability. A new religious Establishment had arisen to interpret the words of Yahweh to the people. And what does Jesus talk about? **Whitewash**. 'Woe to you, scribes and Pharisees, hypocrites! for you are like whitewashed tombs, which outwardly appear beautiful, but within they are full of dead men's bones' (Mt 23:27).

As a good watchman, Jesus had a just perspective on the religious Establishment of his day. Its leaders were quite in favour of prophets – *dead* prophets. 'You build the tombs of the prophets and adorn the monuments of the righteous' (Mt 23:29). But living prophets, those who actually address the people with good news of a living alternative to the way of death, the religious leaders will kill, crucify, scourge and 'persecute from town to town' (Mt 23:34).

Such a stifling of the prophets, Jesus knew, would lead to devastation. 'Your enemies will set up siege-works against you; they will encircle you and hem you in at every point; they will bring you to the ground, you and your children within your walls, and not leave you one stone standing on another' (Lk 19:43–44). This grieved Jesus. If only the people would recognize 'God's moment' which he represented. If only they would come like chicks to the true security of his wings (Mt 23:37). If only they, the Jerusalemites, could set out on 'the way that leads to *shalom*' (Lk 19:42). In Jesus' appeal there is an invitation to change; there is time to change.

But the way of *shalom*, which Jesus lived and into which he invited others, seemed unwise to the leaders of the religious Establishment. Conventional considerations of security dominated their thinking: 'If we let him go on thus, every one will believe in him, and the Romans will come and destroy both our holy place and our nation' (Jn 11:48). So, as a result of a lesser-evil calculation, in an attempt to act responsibly for the *shalom* of the nation, they crucified the prophet whose gaze had penetrated their whitewash. The result, once again, was devastation. Within less than a half century the Jerusalemites, their religious leaders, and their temple were destroyed – by another empire which the early Christians called Babylon, *Rome*.

Prophetic Challenge Today

As we read the prophets and gospels today, these themes continue to reverberate. They are living themes, ringing with the resonance of the Spirit of God who has never stopped striving with men and women. Since Yahweh is not a pocket deity, his message will be uncomfortable for us all. Any of us who speak for peace must expect our vision of *shalom* to be carefully scrutinized.

Not least is this true of those of us who advocate peace through costly reconciliation and nuclear disarmament. We must beware of glib generalizations: if we are genuinely attentive to those with whom we disagree we may find some initial steps of repentance upon which we can both agree. We must also beware of moral shallowness. Ezekiel, it is noteworthy, was not critical solely of his own people; in one striking passage he calls his people's enemy the Babylonians 'the worst of nations' (Ez 7:24). Nor did he despair, even when it appeared that there would be universal rejection of his message and the destruction of all that he had loved. For Yahweh was there, ready, in ways that he could only dimly discern, to bring creativity out of chaos. We cannot be true watchers in the world if we are attuned only to the latest tick of the doomsday clock; we must also, like Ezekiel, listen to the One whom a New Testament Jewish writer calls the 'God of hope' (Rom 15:13).

Other challenges will confront those who seek *shalom* through military strength. Far more than the so-called 'peace movement,' it is the representatives of the Establishment who use the language of peace. How reassuring it all sounds. The motto of the US Strategic Air Command is 'Peace is our Profession'; the MX-missile has been christened the 'Peacekeeper'; Western military policy has been characterized as 'peace through strength'. The nuclear bomb, our Secretary of Defence informs us, has enabled us since 1945 to 'keep the peace'. Some Christian thinkers, not surprisingly, enunciate the same theme in biblical language: a Christian organization which has argued for the siting of cruise missiles in Britain has chosen to call itself *Shalom*.

What would Ezekiel's perspective – Jesus' perspective – be

on this use of language? What would they think of all of the ingenuity and expenditure to which this language leads? In our attempt to discern the word of God for our time, there can be few questions that are more important than these. For the struggle for true peace is one in which we all engage; even the deluded prophets of *shalom* who exasperated Ezekiel genuinely expected Yahweh to deliver it according to their formulae (Ez 13:6).

But sincerity is not enough: all sides cannot be right today any more than they were in Ezekiel's day. Some of us are misreading the world; some of us are mis-hearing Yahweh. If some of us are watchers, others of us are whitewashers.

This is the risk of living – we must make choices, and we may be wrong. Ezekiel's priestly colleagues must have thought that he had gone round the twist; and many of Jesus' critics thought that he had a demon. So, in the competition among prophets that is taking place now, let us not be surprised by misunderstanding and rejection. Let us stand in the councils of Yahweh and listen. Let us be suspicious of easy answers, from any source (including the most respectable); we know, from both Testaments, that whitewash is incompatible with *shalom*. Let us be doubtful of any solution, from Christian or non-Christian, that promises security without repentance and suffering.

Finally, let us never be unaware of our own responsibility. It is not only the Establishment that has a 'responsible approach' to questions of peace and security. They do have their responsibility. But so, as watchers, do we. If they, on the basis of delusive visions, act wrongly with the immense power at their disposal, judgement will rest upon them. If we, on the other hand, do not speak the vision that has been given to us, the blood of the people will be on our hands (Ez 3:19). The skies are heavy, but the hailstones have not yet started to fall. God is giving us time.

Noel Moules

It was a talk given at Festival 1984 that caused the editor of this volume to note Noel Moules' peace commitment. After some correspondence it became clear that for Noel, writing on peace meant writing about Jesus, and so he has in this chapter. In it we are offered a picture of our Lord as He was in the flesh and as He is today among men and women: the true peacemaker.

Noel works with Dave Tomlinson in Team Work, a ministry which serves house churches and fellowships throughout Britain. Living in Southeast London, he directs Team Work's leadership training programme and is involved with others in church planting in the inner-city.

6: Jesus – the Peacemaker

Noel Moules

'Blessed are the peacemakers
for they shall be called children of God'. (Mt 5:9)

As I hear this cry of Jesus it echoes around the corridors of power and the offices of rulers. It sounds across the desks of generals, past armament factories and nuclear missile silos. It reverberates down city streets where millions try to hide their fear behind brave faces. It thunders through the church.

The modern world sees Jesus of Nazareth as irrelevant to the dilemmas of the twentieth century. Most Christians see concern about the nuclear issue as a diversion, even a perversion, of the true thrust of the gospel. Both are mistaken. Without Jesus there can never be peace. The 'shalom' which is central to the gospel proclamation has as its goal, not only changed hearts, but structures of societies harmonised with the heart of God himself.[1]

The focus

Throughout the Church there is an awakening to this cry of Jesus. More and more of us are responding to God's call to be peacemakers and are standing up and speaking out against the nuclear bomb. Brothers and sisters are coming together from different backgrounds with a variety of perceptions and opinions. Some are nuclear pacifists, some are mainstream pacifists, others are taking a stand while still working through questions for themselves. Differences in emphasis between us are not important for we are all learning and discovering the full implications of God's call together. What is important, in fact fundamental, is that it is the person of Jesus who unites us. It is he who fuses us together and sets the pace for the way ahead.

It is to Jesus we are responding, not simply to the horror of a potential holocaust. It is his word that is calling us to action, not simply the crying need of our generation. It is Jesus who gives us our identity. It is in Him that we have been received by adoption to be children of God with a birthright of peacemaking. It is Jesus who gives us our uniqueness. He prevents us from being simply absorbed into the vague mass of ideas that often form destructive undercurrents in the peace movement. It is Jesus who gives us our distinctive values. In Him we see that the root of the nuclear issue is first and foremost spiritual and not simply social, political and economic. It is Jesus who enables us to walk completely free from fear, that fear which lies like a cloud across the nations and has so insidiously polluted much of current political protest. Jesus gives us our strategy. Others pursue utopias, in Jesus we proclaim the kingdom of God upon earth.

The model

In today's world the title 'peacemaker' is adorned by mystic and militant, nonviolent and aggressor alike. However, Jesus calls peacemakers 'children of God'. So if we are to understand what this really means we must look at the one who, as the perfect Son of God is therefore the perfect incarnation of the 'peacemaker'.

We expect peacemakers to focus upon conflict, speak words of reconciliation, search for resolve, and calm troubled situations. This must be true, but the life of Jesus the peacemaker highlights some disturbing contrasts to this simple view. Yes, Jesus does focus upon conflict, but more frequently He himself stands as the focal point of the crisis itself. Jesus moves into people's lives bringing healing, forgiveness and resolve, but he also shatters open situations that superficially appear inoffensive. He deliberately precipi-

tates crisis by his carefully chosen words and actions. He
probes beneath the surface and touches hidden attitudes and
motives that, under camouflage, are seething with hostility.[2]
Jesus well illustrates the saying, 'the only place for the peacemaker is at the centre of the battle field'. But what he alarm-
ingly reveals is that often the peacemaker is required to fire
the opening shot in the conflict. Jesus states this very clearly;

'For crisis I have come into this world'. (Jn 9:39)

'I came to cast fire upon the earth.' (Lk 12:49)

Jesus created conflict with the expressed purpose of
resolving conflict. In being peacemakers after his pattern we
become flashpoints in crisis. We are to be detonators that
explode everything superficial and hypocritical. We are to
be catalysts that create reactions which identify what the true
issues really are. We are to become lightning-rods which
earth the high voltage of conflict in ourselves, by virtue of
our relationship with God. True peacemaking can never be
cosmetic, 'papering over the cracks'. It is radical, reaching
down to the roots of conflict and tearing them out.

'Do not think that I have come to bring peace on earth, I
have not come to bring peace but a sword.' (Mt 10:34)[3]

Only then can healing begin and the wholeness of peace
be born.
In Jesus the way of the peacemaker is best described as
a 'shalom-activist'. We are initiators; making the running,
turning the tide. We have insight; the prophetic eye, seeing
the true nature of things and declaring both warnings and
encouragement. We have patience, yes; but true biblical patience, vibrant with activity, leaving no stone unturned until
a solution is found.[4]
Peacemaking is alive with creativity. It is actively making
peace. It is building a whole new environment in which the
forces of destruction have been transformed into the energized wholeness of shalom. As I watch Jesus the peacemaker
at work I see a craftsman who, from the raw materials of

fear, hatred and violence, creates masterpieces in human lives and circumstances.[5]

Peacemaking emphasises the fact that very hard work is involved. Peace is only brought into being by real effort: sweat, toil and pain. Swords actually have to be beaten into ploughshares.[6] The skills of peacemaking have to be learned. Discipline, sensitivity and maturity are all essential. Let us watch Jesus engaging in conflict situations. This will show us exactly what is required as we embrace a peace apprenticeship with the master.

'Strength within.'

Peacemakers cannot bring peace without first finding peace within themselves. All conflict and violence, from personal to international, has to do with the issues of 'identity' and 'security'. It was Jesus' knowledge of who He was, His origin and destiny, that gave Him identity and security. In the closing hours before His execution it is said of Him:–

'Jesus knowing the Father had given all things into his hands, and that he was coming from God and was going to God, rose from supper, laid aside his garments, girded himself with a towel and washed the disciples' feet.'[7]

Here is a man secure. Jesus stands in the teeth of conflict with poise and stature. The man of dynamic tranquillity. Fearless in the face of the mob, whether threatening to hurl him over the cliff at Nazareth,[8] stone Him in Jerusalem,[9] or arrest him in Gethsemene.[10] Throughout his ministry, from the temptations in the wilderness,[11] to His agonising prayer in the garden,[12] Jesus faced attack at His roots. If He could be broken here everything else would crumble. But He was established. Attack could only prove that He was not vulnerable.[13]

In speaking out against nuclear weapons the first line of resistance is always people's insecurity. If we do not recognise this we are building on sand. Our progress in the political arena will only be as strong as the security people feel within themselves. Standing against the fears by which people are haunted is one of the essential contributions Christians make to the peace movement.

Under threat of stoning, Jesus prepares to visit Lazarus. The disciples fear for his life, and their own. Jesus' reply sets these issues in perfect perspective:–

'Are there not twelve hours in the day? If anyone walks in the day he does not stumble because he sees the light of this world. But if he walks in the night he stumbles because the light is not in him.' (Jn 11:9)

There is both the time and opportunity to do the work ahead. But situations must be exploited because there is not unlimited time. As children of the light we can walk with confidence and security, even when it is dark and others have to grope their way ahead.

Peacemakers are vulnerable, 'lambs in the midst of wolves'.[14] Our stand will provoke hostility, and attempt to uncover any weakness we may have. It is not enough to have clear factual arguments at our fingertips. The first and sharpest line of attack in any debate about nuclear weapons will be the challenge to our personal security:–

'Would you really leave our nation defenceless?'
'What about your loved ones, your children?'

Reasoned rebuffs to these questions are not difficult, but it is simply not enough to win the debate intellectually. People soon know whether or not these issues have been finally settled in our spirits. It is here the battle is really fought and won.

Cutting to the roots

Jesus' declaration of the truth launched a radical challenge to the traditional ideas of his day. In its many forms tradition presented the most hostile and sustained attack upon him. Breaking the Sabbath by healing and working, ignoring the rituals of handwashing, prayer and fasting, exercising his divine authority to forgive sins or mixing with undesirables. Jesus scandalized his contemporaries' framework of thinking.[15]

Tradition is a strange phenomena. It clearly plays an important part in the human consciousness, yet time and again it displays a hideous capacity for masking the very values it claims to preserve. Tradition is a servant of truth, but we in our insecure search for identity persist in clinging blindly to it rather than returning to source. Instead, we weave a web of ideas that replaces the truth; it becomes an idol sacred and untouchable. Where tradition preserved truth, Jesus affirmed it;[16] where it did not, he cut it to the ground.[17]

It is established traditional attitudes that offer strongest resistence to our stand against nuclear weapons. Most people are unable to see the madness of the old ways of thinking in this era of new military technology. As Einstein said after that development of the Bomb, 'Everything has changed except our way of thinking'. Like Jesus we must cut through to the root and declare the truth.

We will find, like Jesus did, that any attack on tradition is always met by the challenge, 'What right do you have to speak like this?'[18] Jesus made it clear that his authority rested upon his relationship with God, evidenced by his actions and the obvious truth of his words.[19] As Christian peace-makers we have no other ground to stand on. We speak because God has spoken and we cannot keep silent. Words must be matched by character and lifestyle. Arguments must find their strength in the quietness and confidence of clear honest presentation and conviction.

Jesus caused a dilemma. His attacks on tradition aroused so much hatred that the people wanted to kill him, while at the same time everyone had to admit that the things he did were wonderful![20] He is our example.

The weapon of wisdom

Watching Jesus engage in conflict situations is breath-taking. Every word and action is spontaneous and unpredict-able. His message is packed with paradox, yet remains consistent and without compromise. Jesus meets every crisis with profound wisdom. Not the usual blend of common sense, broad experience and mental agility, but inspired insight and penetrating perception, radical and ruthless while at the same time disarming and winsome. Jesus wields words like a master swordsman and moves into conflict with all the skill of a warrior in hand-to-hand combat. But he does not fight to win, rather to proclaim the truth and expose evil. His opponents may be silenced[21] but they are never humiliated. A door to God's kingdom is always left open to them.[22] Some of Jesus' most powerful statements about God's love come in response to the most bitter attacks against him.[23]

Whenever hostility closes around Jesus we see him carefully assessing the situation before he responds: the voice from the crowd trying to entangle him with trick questions;[24] a group of religious leaders drawing him into debate to trap him into publicly discrediting himself and giving them a basis for legal action.[25] Only once he has weighed their words and discerned their spirit and intent does he make his response. He is the man in control because he is the man who listens.

'Be wise as serpents . . .'[26] Jesus is master of 'kingdom cunning'. Displays of spellbinding wisdom which not only resolve the issue, thrown like a gauntlet at his feet, but expose the motives of his attacker. The woman caught in the very act of adultery is a powerful example. In Jewish law an open and closed case. However, when Jesus was through, it had been turned on its head; the offender walked away forgiven and the accusers were confessing their guilt![27]

Jesus always turned the full force of the attack back upon his accusers. Like a wrestler using his opponents own strength to defeat him by catching him off balance. Aggressive questions were often parried by another of his own:

'Was John's baptism from heaven or from men?'[28]

His purpose was not to destroy his opponents, as they wished to do to him, but rather to force them to reveal their true feelings and so discover if there was any ground upon which to build. It was also often his practice to pick up the very accusation which had been thrown at him, lying like some half-brick on the ground, and use it as an object lesson from which to illustrate truth:—

'Show me a coin . . . Whose inscription is upon it? . . . Give to Ceasar what is Ceasar's and to God what is God's.' (Mt 22:19–21)

Whenever Jesus sensed there was no real interest in his words he would give his attackers no satisfaction. He remained silent.[29] He would not share the subtle treasures of the kingdom of God with people of brute attitude:—

'Don't give what is holy to dogs,
don't cast your pearls before swine.' (Mt 7:6)

For Jesus a conflict had to count for something or else it was a useless and dangerous diversion. He illustrates this well on the occasions when he had to face a hostile mob. Sometimes he defused the tension by his teaching,[30] at other times he simply walked off and left them standing.[31] On other occasions wisdom dictated that he hide in the Temple[32] or escape across Jordan.[33] On each occasion he had to decide whether or not what faced him was in fact a creative crisis. His work was not to be endangered or frustrated. Nevertheless, when the time was right he would allow himself to be engulfed by the mob as the means of winning the greatest victory of all.[34]

'Be harmless as doves . . .'[35] For all its penetrating ruthlessness, the wisdom of Jesus is marked by an uncanny gentleness. Its razor sharpness was honed by love. His opponents were never belittled or manipulated by fear. Even men sent to arrest him were charmed by his gracious words.[36] In the heat of the moment his motives were always pure,[37] never corrupted by blind passion, insecurity or self-interest. He is the inspiration for words to be written later in the New Testament era:—

'The wisdom from above is first pure, then peaceable, gentle, open to reason, full of mercy and good fruits, without uncertainty or insincerity.' (Ja 3:17)

We must learn to use wisdom as Jesus did, for example when on trial before Caiaphas and Pilate, standing amid conflict with utter poise.[38] Notice the skilful balance of listening, answering, questioning and silence. Conflict is both an opportunity to be exploited and a snare to be avoided. And wisdom has been promised:–

'Relax . . . I will give you a mouth and wisdom.'[39]

Stand up and proclaim[40]

Jesus was an activist. All the major incidents of conflict in his life sprang from moments of bold public demonstration and declaration. His work was more than going about doing good to individuals and engaging in personal dialogue. It demanded taking a public stand which was calculated to bring him into conflict with the political forces of his day.

At Nazareth Jesus read from the 'messianic manifesto' in Isaiah with its promise of release to the poor, the imprisoned and the enslaved.[41] In him these words would be fulfilled. There was uproar.[42] Later at Jerusalem he rode into the city in kingly style with the crowd shouting royal acclaim. The political implications of his actions were lost on no one – the religious leaders were enraged.[43] Following this Jesus entered the Temple, drove out the traders and restored the courtyards as a place of worship. Would the next stop be the Roman garrison? The plans to kill him were finalised.[44]

Jesus gives a very important place to protest. People's attention must be gained, issues highlighted, truth declared, attitudes challenged and decisions demanded. Our protest, however, must be distinctive. It must be prophetic proclamation rather than mere public show. A vehicle for God's word not the fruit of fear and frustration. It is a risky area. The method and the moment are critical. The medium becomes the message. Jesus could have leapt from the Temple tower or turned stones into bread;[45] it would have been wrong. He chose instead to read from prophecy, ride on a donkey and close down a market; but the timing and impact was electric. Our protests must be acted prophecies. In removing the money changers, the issue is not whether he used the whip on anyone, but the message, 'God is straightening things out and he is beginning here!' No one present had any doubts about what was being proclaimed.

Jesus is the man of explosive calm. He displayed zeal and passion, anger and indignation as he hungered and thirsted after righteousness. His emotions, as well as his words and actions, communicated his message.

'The zeal of the Lord of Hosts will consume me.'[46]

But he was in perfect control of his emotions as well as events. Meekness was his hallmark.[47] Every impulse rested under perfect discipline. We must feel our message as well as proclaim it. It is this that brings conviction. Nevertheless, to feel without control leads to violence, while to proclaim without feeling spawns legalism. Jesus showed the perfect balance.

Embracing the cost

In the flickering torchlight of Gethsemane, a kiss is the signal for the arrest to take place. A sword flash. A cry. Blood poured from the head of a man in the official party. It was a moment history has witnessed a thousand times. The spark to ignite revolt and insurrection. But before events could follow their predictable course of bloodshed, a voice rang out in the darkness and silenced the melee. 'No more of this!' All eyes fixed upon Jesus, as his disciples dropped their weapons and he touched and healed the severed ear.[48] It was a revolutionary moment.

The path of the peacemaker leads inevitably into the eye of the storm. Jesus made it no secret that walking his path of truth and righteousness was destined to provoke the forces of hostility, bringing pain and division.[49] Only hours before he had warned that the crisis was about to climax:–

'Let him who has no sword sell his mantle and buy one.'[50]

He was not choosing the zealot option as his disciples mistakenly presumed. Rather he was preparing their minds for another way; more painful, radical, and remedial than any other. There can be no peace without a price and the price is always self-sacrifice. Peacemaking is a redemptive act; the peacemaker bears the cost within himself. For this reason the path from the garden led inevitably to Golgotha.

'For the Son of man came also not to be served but to serve, and to give his life as a ransom for many.'[51]

Self-sacrifice alone is not enough. It is the spirit of sacrifice. The price of peace can only be fully paid when the currency is love. Only love can embrace the forces of hostility and change them:–

'Love your enemies and pray for those who persecute you so that you may be children of your Father in heaven' [ie. 'peacemakers']. (Mt 5:44)

Jesus could touch the wounds of conflict and bring healing, but to deal with the roots demanded his life. Violence drove the spikes into his wrists but it was love that held his arms to the scaffold.

The tools of peacemaking which Jesus has placed into our hands – love, prayer, truth, wisdom, courage, self-sacrifice and destiny – seem dwarfed by the spectres of the nuclear age. But energized by the Spirit and focused, under God's guidance, upon critical situations, they are invincible.

With joy[52]

Look into the face of some peace protesters. Behind the slogans and the placards, the eyes are often sad, the voices edged with anger, frustration and fear. Unfortunately it is a stark contrast to the style of Jesus.

'Oh the joy of being peacemakers . . .' (Mt 5:9)

This captures the spirit of his words. The thrill of working shoulder to shoulder with the purposes of God. We will feel the sharp winds of conflict, but:

'Happy are you when people revile you . . . rejoice and be glad for your reward is great in heaven.' (Mt 5:12)

Our voices will often resound with seriousness and anger, but we must never lose the lightness in our step. There will be tears, but laughter is never very far away.[53] We are children of the hope and of the promise. What a privilege to be a peacemaker and follow in his steps. With the sound of his words ringing in our ears:

'Be of good cheer, I have overcome the world!'[54]

What else can we do but sing . . . and roll up our sleeves.

References

1. Ep 1:10
2. cf. Lk 4:16–30
3. cf. Lk 12:51
4. cf. Lk 15:8
5. cf. Mk 5:1–20
6. Is 2:4; Mic 4:3
7. Jn 13:3–4
8. Lk 4:29
9. Jn 10:31
10. Jn 18:4
11. Lk 4:1–2
12. Mt 26:36
13. Jn 14:30
14. Lk 10:3
15. cf. Mt 12–15; Lk 5–6
16. Mt 13:52; 23:2
17. cf. Mt 23:13–15
18. cf. Mt 21:23
19. Jn 10:37–38
20. Jn 10:31–33; Mt 12:9–14
21. Mt 22:34
22. cf. Mt 23:37; 7:36–50
23. cf. Lk 15 esp. 1–2
24. Mt 22:15–16
25. Jn 8:6
26. Mt 10:16
27. Jn 7:53–8:11
28. Mk 11:30
29. Jn 19:8–9
30. Jn 7:48
31. Lk 4:30
32. Jn 12:36
33. Jn 10:39–40
34. Mk 15:11–14
35. Mt 10:16
36. Jn 7:48 cf. Lk 19:47
37. Mt 5:8
38. cf. Jn 18:17–19:16; Lk 22:63–23:12
39. Lk 21:13–15; Mt 10:19
40. Jn 7:37
41. Is 61:1–2
42. Lk 4:16–30
43. Lk 19:36–40
44. Mk 11:15–19
45. Lk 4:1–13
46. Jn 2:17; Ps 69:9
47. Mt 5:5
48. Lk 22:47–53
49. Mt 5:10; 10:24–25, 34–39; Lk 12:51; Jn 7:7
50. Lk 22:36–38
51. Mk 10:45
52. Is 55:12
53. Lk 6:21
54. Jn 16:33

Richard Bauckham

While the Book of Revelation is probably the most misunderstood book of the Bible, it is probably also the most misused one. Richard Bauckham helps us to read the book with fresh understanding, shedding our Lindsay*-ised interpretations to recapture more of its original intention and relevance for contemporary issues. And certainly no other issues are more key to the book than ultimate destruction and political manifestations of power.

Richard Bauckham is a leading biblical scholar and theologian who lectures in theology at University of Manchester.

* Hal Lindsay, author of *The Late Great Planet Earth*.

7: Approaching the Apocalypse

Richard Bauckham

Some readers will detect a *double meaning* in my title, since the word 'Apocalypse,' which originally meant 'revelation', is therefore an alternative name for the New Testament book of Revelation. But the word now often refers to a cataclysmic end of human history, such as might happen in a nuclear holocaust.

There are Christian circles in which these two meanings come very close together: the book of Revelation is thought to prophesy that human history will end in a nuclear holocaust, which is now in the near future. My conviction is that that interpretation of the Apocalypse arises from a misguided way of reading the book. In this essay I shall try to outline a more satisfactory way of 'approaching the Apocalypse' (the book), in the hope that this may also help us in our approach to the possibility of a nuclear holocaust.

Understanding the language and imagery

The book of Revelation is a difficult book to understand. Rather like Dante's *Divine Comedy* or Spenser's *Faerie Queene*, it is a complex literary work which depends, for its effect and meaning, on a wide range of symbols and allusions. Catching the allusions and grasping the significance of the symbols would have been easier for contemporaries than it is for us. They knew the world in which John wrote, they read the literature he read, they understood the literary conventions of the type of literature he wrote. We need to learn about those things in order to understand his work, just as we do if we want to appreciate Dante or Milton or even James Joyce.

But understanding the background to an author's work is still not understanding his work itself. We still need to appreciate the creative use he makes of the materials and the literary conventions he took over. Shakespeare used the conventions of Elizabethan drama and plundered the plots, sometimes even the words, of previous stories and plays, but his creative imagination made something quite new and much greater out of these materials. Similarly John used the literary conventions and traditions of apocalyptic literature, and therefore a familiarity with (among other things) other apocalypses from ancient Judaism and Christianity can help us to understand his work. But his inspired creative imagination also shaped his work into something rather distinctive, not just a typical apocalypse. Thus, to understand the Apocalypse, we need to be informed about the sources of its symbols and allusions – in the literature, culture and history of its time – and also to study the creative use John makes of them.

Fortunately for us, one of the major sources of John's language and imagery is readily accessible, even if we do not know it as well as John knew it and evidently expected his readers to know it. This is the Old Testament. The Apocalypse is saturated with verbal allusions to the Old Testament, which John expects us to recognize and which are often the key to his meaning. Among his Old Testament sources, John had certain key texts (such as Psalm 2 and Daniel 7) to which a network of allusions throughout the book refers. He also derived from the Old Testament some of the controlling images which run through his work, such as the new Exodus, the fall of Babylon, the conflict of Elijah and Jezebel, and the holy war. In all this John is engaged in a creative Christian interpretation of the Old Testament, and we must be alert to the ways in which he adapts and transmutes the significance of his material. The new Exodus, for example, is one in which Jesus Christ is the passover lamb. The holy war is a struggle in which witness and martyrdom are the means of victory.

John also uses mythological images which had strong associations in the world of his day. The serpent or the dragon is a good example of a symbol which had biblical roots (Gen. 3:14–15; Isa. 27:1), but also wide cultural resonances in his readers' minds, owing to its prominence in pagan mythology and religion. Another type of contemporary allusion is the idea of invasion from the East (Rev. 9:13–19; 16:12). Here John is taking up a very real political fear in the Roman Empire in the first century, since the threat of invasion from the Parthian Empire of the East was widely felt. (Clearly it carried the same kind of overtones of conquest by a cruel and alien civilization as the threat of Russian invasion has for many Europeans today.) When John pictures the kings of the East in alliance with 'the beast who was and is not and is to ascend from the pit' (17:12), he is echoing the contemporary myth which pictured the hatred tyrant Nero returning one day at the head of the Parthian hordes to conquer the Roman Empire. In these kinds of ways John's images echo and play on the facts, the fears, the imaginings and the myths of his contemporaries, in order to transmute them into elements of his own Christian meaning.

Once we begin to appreciate the sources and the rich associations of John's imagery, we realise that it cannot be read as literal description, but must be read for its theological meaning and its contemporary resonances. Consider, for example, the descriptions of the plagues of the seven trumpets (chs. 8–9) and the seven bowls (ch. 16). The contents of these plagues are intended to suggest, among other things, the plagues of Egypt, the fall of Jericho, the locust-army of Joel's prophecy, the contemporary fear of invasion by the Parthian cavalry, and very possibly the eruption of Vesuvius, which had recently terrified the Mediterranean world.

To observe, as some modern Christians have, that some of the description sounds a little like the effects of nuclear war is quite beside John's point. He wrote to be understood by his contemporaries. He took their worst experiences and worst fears of war and natural disaster, blew them up to apocalyptic proportions, and cast them in biblically allusive terms. His intention was to say: the coming judgment of the world will be either – depending on your response – a realization of your worst nightmares, or a new Exodus through which the people of God must pass to the promised land. To associate John's imagery with a nuclear holocaust may help us to grasp its significance, because this is our equivalent to the nightmares of first-century people. But this does not mean that John's imagery can be taken as a prediction of a nuclear holocaust, any more than it was meant to be a prediction of a Parthian invasion or a volcanic eruption.

When one compares John's Apocalypse with the other examples we have of the literary genre of apocalypse, one of the striking differences which emerges is the remarkable extent of the visual imagery in John's work. The other apocalypses provide precedents and even sources for the type of imagery John uses, but not for its profusion. I think that the powerful visual impact of the Apocalypse must be connected, in part, with its purpose of providing an alternative vision of the world for readers who found the contemporary Roman pagan vision of the world difficult to resist.

John's readers, who lived in the great cities of the province of Asia, were constantly confronted with *images* of the Roman vision of the world. Architecture, iconography, statues, religious and political ceremony created powerful visual impressions of Roman imperial power and of the splendour of pagan religion. John therefore provides a series of prophetic counter-images which impress on his readers a different vision of the world: how the world looks from the heaven to which John is caught up in chapter 4. The visual power of his work effects a kind of purging of the Christian imagination, re-fashions the pagan images into a strikingly different shape, and refurbishes the Christian imagination with alternative visions of how the world is and will be. In chapter 17, for example, John's readers share his vision of a woman. She is the goddess Roma, in all her glory, a stunning personification of the civilization of Rome. But as John sees her, she is also a Roman *prostitute*, a seductive whore and a scheming witch, with biblical overtones of the harlot queen Jezebel to reinforce the impression. In this way, John's readers are able to perceive something of Rome's true character, – her moral corruption behind the enticing propagandist illusions of Rome that they constantly encountered in the world.

The Apocalypse as a circular letter

This emphasis on what the Apocalypse could have meant to its first readers, as a key to its interpretation, may be questioned. 'Surely John was really writing for future generations?' you may be saying. In reply, I would point to one of the surest guides to John's intentions: the literary form in which he chose to write. The Apocalypse is not only an apocalypse, it is an apocalypse in the form of a circular *letter*, as his opening in 1:4–5 makes quite clear. In other words, John wrote his apocalypse as a letter to the seven churches of Asia. The whole of the Apocalypse is addressed to those seven first-century churches, in exactly the same way as 1 Corinthians is addressed to the first-century church in Corinth.

Of course, it is also relevant to us, just as 1 Corinthian is. But just as we have to read 1 Corinthians as written in the first instance to the church at Corinth, and cannot hope to understand it if we imagine it addressed directly to us, so we have to read the Apocalypse as written to the seven churches of Asia. This alone should be sufficient to show us that the Apocalypse cannot tell us whether, in literal chronological terms, we are approaching Armageddon. There is a sense in which it told John's first readers that *they* were approaching Armageddon, and that message holds good for us in the same sense – but not as a literal prediction.

John writes a circular letter to the seven churches, and within it he includes a short message from the risen Christ specifically to each of the seven churches (chs. 2–3). Thus, for example, the Christians at Ephesus would read the whole book as addressed to them, but they would find in the passage addressed *specifically* to them (2:1–7) a kind of key to the way in which they should read the rest of the book. It would help them to identify the ways in which the rest of the book was relevant to them, which might be different from the ways in which it was relevant to, say, the church at Smyrna.

We should therefore think of these seven messages to the churches not as self-contained letters (as is so often done), but as seven different *introductions* to the rest of the Apocalypse. In writing his Apocalypse John had in mind seven rather different church situations, and the seven messages therefore provide seven different points of entry to the main themes of his work. Not only did this help his first readers; it can also help us. The seven messages to the churches provide us with seven different perspectives from which to read the Apocalypse. Thus we might find it useful to pick out the church whose situation seems most to resemble our modern church situation and to try reading the Apocalypse from the perspective provided for them.

I do not have space here to illustrate in detail how the Apocalypse can be read from the various perspectives of the seven messages to the churches. It depends on picking up the links between the themes and images of the messages to the churches and those of the rest of the book. One rather obvious example must suffice to make the point. At Thyatira, a professing Christian prophetess was teaching that Christians could participate without qualms of conscience in the idolatrous religious practices which were part and parcel of the thriving commercial life of the city (2:20). In calling her Jezebel, after the Old Testament queen who seduced Israel to idolatry in the time of Elijah, John is not simply using an abusive nickname, but proposing that his readers at Thyatira see in their situation a serious parallel to the great crisis of true and false religion in Israel at the time of Elijah. Then in chapter 17 these readers would encounter another, more formidable Jezebel, the harlot queen, drunk with the blood of the saints and deceiving the nations with her sorceries (17:1–6; 18:23; cf. 1 Kings 18:13; 2 Kings 9:22). This Jezebel is the pagan city of Rome, whose trade and commerce were a means of enticing the nations into the sphere of her political religion, in whose name Christians were put to death. Linking the two Jezebels, the Christians at Thyatira would be able to see that their prophetess was, so to speak, the local representative of the harlot of Babylon within their own church life. Through her the seductive power of the alliance of commerce and idolatrous religion was penetrating their church and threatening their own faithfulness to Christ. Thus the theme of chapter 17, which had a general applicability to all of John's readers, gained a special relevance to the concrete circumstances of the church at Thyatira.

So the function of the seven messages is to angle the message of the Apocalypse as a whole to the situations in which the churches found themselves when John wrote to them. At the other end of the Apocalypse, chapters 21–22 portray the churches as they are to become: the Bride of Christ and the New Jerusalem. In between, chapters 4–20 are, so to speak, the bridge which the churches must cross from the state in which they are to the destiny they must inherit. Those chapters portray the conflict into which John's churches are being plunged and in which they must be victorious if they are to become the Bride. Since not only those seven churches, but all churches, are called to become the Bride, the Apocalypse has something to say to all churches. But we must not forget that its route to the New Jerusalem begins not where we are, but where those seven churches of first-century Asia Minor were.

The Apocalypse as a prophecy

As well as being an apocalypse and a letter, the book of Revelation is a prophecy (1:3; 22:7). The meaning of 'prophecy' here certainly includes an element of prediction ('what must soon take place': 1:1; 22:6). But the prediction is closely linked to a prophetic *discernment* of the true nature of the historical situation and a prophetic *demand* for an appropriate response. John's prophecy is given to the churches to enable *them* to 'prophesy' to the world (cf. 11:2), since John identifies prophecy with 'bearing the witness of Jesus' (19:10; cf. 1:2). In other words, they were to bear witness before the world in the way that Jesus did. Their prophetic insight into their situation and where they are heading will enable John's churches to bear their witness faithfully.

John's prophetic insight into his contemporary situation comes through his being enabled to see it in a *heavenly* perspective and in an *eschatological* perspective. John is taken up into heaven (4:1) so that he can see from 'behind the scenes,' so to speak, what is really going on in the events of his time – how they look from the divine standpoint. He is also transported into the final future (cf. 21:10), so that he can see the present situation from the perspective of what its final outcome must be, in God's ultimate purpose for human history. From the insight which is thus given him in the Spirit, John calls on his readers to *discern* the realities of their situation and to see through the illusions of the pagan Roman view of the world. The theme of discerning true and false realities, truth and deceit, runs through the whole of the Apocalypse.

The great issue was where real power lay in the world of John's time. The apparently vast power of the beast deceived the world into thinking him divine (13:4, 14–15). He was worshipped because he seemed irresistible in power and influence. We should remember how very difficult it must have been for Christians, as a tiny minority without power or influence, to take any other view of the matter – but John wants them to see through the illusion of the beast's power and deity. He had, of course, a kind of power: the power of the sword against all who resisted him (13:15). But the real truth – the heavenly and eschatological truth – was that the Lamb *had* conquered and *will* conquer (5:5; 17:14), that the kingdom of this world will become the kingdom of God and the Lamb (11:15).

The reality of the situation, then, was that of a cosmic conflict, in which the beast seemed to be winning. John's churches needed to see their day-to-day lives and decisions as part of the great cosmic struggle of good and evil which the Apocalypse depicts. They needed to discern the real alignments in the conflict since all too easily Christians could find themselves taking the beast's side, compromising with and conniving at evil. So John's great dramatic images of evil – the dragon, the beasts, the whore – not only portray the great international forces of evil, but also link these forces to the local situations of the churches depicted in the seven messages.

From discernment comes John's call for 'endurance and faithfulness' (13:10; 14:12), or faithful witness to the point of death (12:11). In other words – in the imagery of the holy war which pervades the book – Christians are to enlist in the Lamb's army, to fight and to conquer the beast, and thereby to win through to the New Jerusalem. The beast fights by violence and deceit; Christians fight the Lamb's way, by suffering witness to the truth.

But prophetic discernment of true reality means precisely that the *real* victory is through suffering witness. It is part of the beast's illusion that sheer violence wins, and so in the Roman view of the world, the martyrdom of the saints is a victory for the beast. But from the heavenly and eschatological perspective, the sacrificial witness of the Lamb and his followers serves to expose the falsity of the Roman world and its values, winning the real victory. John's deliberately ambivalent use of the language of conquest and victory constantly makes this point (5:5; 6:2; 11:8; 12:11; 13:7; 15:2; 17:14).

The beast conquers, the Lamb conquers, the saints conquer: whose is the real victory? John's great prophetic images invited his readers to see the matter from a perspective radically different from that of the beast whose propaganda was all around them. Sharing John's prophetic discernment they could then respond to the call to conquer and therefore receive the promise for those who conquer which climaxes each of the seven messages to the churches (2:7, 11, 17, 26; 3:5, 12, 21). By thus following the Lamb in his way of victory they would find their way through the conflict of chapters 4–20 to the fulfilment of the promised New Jerusalem (21:7).

Approaching the nuclear holocaust

We cannot mechanically transpose the Apocalypse's message for its original readers into our own situation. But if we take the trouble to understand both their situation and ours, the similarities and the differences, the Apocalypse can help us to gain prophetic discernment into the threat of the nuclear holocaust. In this final section, I can offer no more than a few suggestions as to how this can happen.

The most obvious point of contact between our situation

and that of the Apocalypse is the threat of judgment on the whole civilized world. Just as John blew up contemporary fears of disaster into nightmarish images of apocalyptic catastrophe, so I think we would not be wrong to take the nightmarish images of nuclear holocaust and nuclear winter, which are now constantly being presented to us in both scientific and imaginative terms, quite seriously as a warning of judgment on our world. Moreover, the Apocalypse's hints that evil is *self*-destructive, bringing down its own judgment on itself and that the beast represents a cult of violent power which in the end destroys the civilization which rests on it (17:16). These are hints which come into their own in the face of the kind of judgment which hangs over us now.

However, it is important to observe *what follows from* the threat of judgment in Revelation for its first readers and for us. There is, first, the need for discernment, in order to identify the real evils which are calling forth the threat of judgment. To penetrate the illusions the beast propagates and to discern the realities of international and local situations can be as hard for us, in the nuclear age, as it was for Christians in the first-century Roman Empire. The ability to see nuclear weapons not simply as potentially disastrous, but as the hideous moral evil they are, is not given to many people today – or not given to them for long. A clear and steady view of the sheer demonic evil of nuclear weapons is difficult to maintain because of the power of the beast's illusion that might is right. Deceit and illusion are also prevalent in the images of the world promoted by Western propaganda about the East and by Eastern propaganda about the West. Contemporary ideology and propaganda, of which not even the peace movement is free, need to be constantly exposed, and to be countered by an alternative, truly Christian view of the world.

Discernment always leads, secondly, to Christian repentance of complicity in the evils discerned, and this involves taking a stand against them. 'Come out of her, my people' (Rev. 18:4) refers, metaphorically, not to a sectarian withdrawal from the world, but to a dissociation which witnesses against the evils of the world. Within the church, where (as with Jezebel at Thyatira) the beast's propaganda can also make considerable inroads, repentance means taking a stand against his lies and his influence.

Thirdly, from the threat of judgment there follows, in Revelation, the church's task of prophetic witness to the world. Biblical announcements of judgment are never fatalistic, but sound a note of warning and a call to repentance. This is no less true of the Apocalypse, which depicts God delaying his judgment so that the church can bear its prophetic witness (chs. 10–11), which is by no means doomed to failure (11:13).

The Apocalypse cannot tell us whether there will be a nuclear holocaust, but it can help us to know how to respond to the threat of one. In the face of that threat, its final message to us presents the possibility of confidence and hope for those who view the world from the heavenly and eschatological perspectives. God is sovereign (ch. 4), the Lamb has conquered (ch. 5), and however dark the immediate future (chs. 6–16), God will build his new Jerusalem on the new earth (ch. 21). This is not the 'I'm-all-right-Jack' confidence of Christians who believe that the world is inevitably doomed to nuclear destruction but that they will be raptured out of it first. Quite the contrary, it is a confidence which leads to that very costly kind of witness which John urges on his readers: following the Lamb wherever he goes (14:4).

Oliver O'Donovan

It was after a weekend of intense debate and discussion that Oliver O'Donovan stepped up to the pulpit and began to preach the following sermon. The weekend, sponsored by the London Institute for Contemporary Christianity, brought together evangelical Christians of all points of view, but who together sought a 'Christian mind on the arms race'. He knew all would not agree with him.

Since that weekend in 1982, Oliver O'Donovan, Professor of Moral Theology at Oxford, has become increasingly noted for his opposition to nuclear weapons. He, together with Ron Sider, participated in a debate on the 'just war theory', published by Grove Booklets, and also wrote another Grove Booklet entitled 'In Pursuit of a Christian View of War'.

In this chapter, O'Donovan explores the politics of the Apocalypse – humanity's last flight from God – and challenges us to consider the place of the faithful in relation to the beast.

8: Humanity's Last Flight from God

Oliver O'Donovan

War has always carried with it a suggestion of apocalypse. Those who find themselves living through the nightmare of war, have always caught a glimpse of the stars falling from their places and the sun and the moon turning to blood, of the end of cosmic order, the stability of creation itself upturned, the heavens rolled up as a garment. That war should open our eyes to this possibility, should make us tremble at the impermanence of human beings and nature alike, is not peculiar to our age. But our age has seen this suggestion become extraordinarily explicit. That which has always been a hint which humankind has discerned behind war has now become a bald statement of fact about war. The nuclear weapon has concretized that which only prophets and poets saw in war: it has given it a statistical definition and clarity; it has made it something on which we have to count in our ordinary calculations.

What we are all struggling for first is to understand this fact, and to understand ourselves in the light of it. So far from it being true that the concrete and the factual is easily grasped by us, the metaphysical and theological only with difficulty: it is clear to me that the 'facts' of our nuclear situation are virtually impossible for any of us to take account of. We continue to think and act as though they weren't there, because we don't know how to take apocalypse into consideration. We will find that we consistently return to the scale of things with which we feel able to cope, excluding all those big things – although they may be human artefacts – which are too big for mere human beings to take into consideration. Our first task is to learn to *think* what we hear, to understand what it means.

We will do that only in the light of Scripture, because only there can we find the meaning of the apocalyptic threat of history interpreted for us in terms that we can grasp in faith: the coming of the Son of Man, whom we have known in his flesh, with great glory. I want to share with you some approaches to understanding which are given to us in the Book of Revelation. I would like to transcend the controversy that has marked the debate among Christians – not unhealthy or bitter controversy, I think, but disagreement nonetheless. I would also have liked to have been positive and practical about making peace. But I do not know how to be practical without presuming a certain understanding of our situation; and I do not know how to suggest an understanding of it without causing some readers to disagree with me – I could only be vapid and vacuous if I tried. And so instead I shall attempt to safeguard unity by resting on the visions of John the Seer, so that we will all be in possession of our heritage in the Word of God, the heritage to which we are answerable; so that *my* vision of where we now stand is itself subjected to John's vision and answerable to it.

Humankind faced with Apocalypse

Three pictures of humankind's approach to cosmic apocalypse:

(1) In Revelation 6, we see in the sequence of seals the progress of history as a progress of war: from the first free adventurous spirit of its beginning, as the rider goes out 'conquering and to conquer', to the slaughter, to the economic chaos and disruption, to the horrors of pestilence which follow, to the terrible injustices wrought against the righteous and innocent, to the moment of the sixth seal at which this cheerful and spirited adventure of the rider on the white horse with a bow and arrows had led to cosmic disruption. The powers of nature are disturbed, and the annihilating

forces which cosmic order holds at bay are let loose. And at
this moment the kings and the politicians and the generals
call on the mountains and the rocks to fall on them. Cosmic
destruction is taken into their project, it becomes part of
their ambition. Why? Because only by laying hold of the
end of nature and pulling it down on themselves, mastering
it even in their own self-destruction, can they hide from its
true meaning as divine judgement. Seizing control of the
apocalypse is humanity's last flight from God – a flight into
suicide, we may say, and that not trivially, for suicide, too,
is in its intention an act of destroying the world and accusing
God.

To me this picture illuminates certain things that are
important about the *project* of strategic nuclear weapons: to
let loose the self-destructive forces of nature that are held in
bay by God's providential will and to master them, bringing
them into our control even if it be to invoke closure on the
world which is the God-given theatre of our existence. This,
according to John the Seer, is where the cheerful, knightly
projects of war were bound to lead.

(2) In Revelation 13:1ff., the devil summons from the
abyss, which is where God has relegated those demonic
forces to which he has said 'No' in establishing the
firmaments, a force (represented as a beast) which will play
a political role in human affairs. John, to the great embarrassment of theologians, will identify this beast concretely as the
ruler of an empire based on the city he calls 'Babylon' which
sits on seven hills: probably Nero. And this is truly astonishing: that the forces of chaos can be turned by Satan to
form a concrete political order, together with an ideology,
the creation of the second beast who acts as a pseudo-prophet
for the first beast. John regards this as the great miracle of
evil, a parody of the Incarnation; and the Trinity of evil, the
devil and the two beasts, is a parody of the Holy Trinity.
In political form, chaos and destruction are made manifest
as order, and men and women worship it. Of course they
do! To them it looks like a resurrection from the dead, a
resurrection of political life from the death of war – but in
fact it is only a parody.

In this picture I find illuminated the fact that the forces of ultimate destruction in our age were summoned up to effect what appeared to be a worthy political goal. The point of nuclear deterrence was to establish and secure a political order without war, protected by the ultimate threat of total chaos. When did humankind first dream that by invoking as servant the ultimate powers of cosmic destruction we could fashion a secure kingdom of peace in which we would be prosperous? Long, long ago. It is the dream given to him by the devil; and John the Seer saw it acted out in the form of an idolatrous empire. In our time we have been visited by another form of the same dream.

(3) In Revelation 18 we learn something of the character of this political order, the life of Babylon. It is a culture of unbounded splendour, economic affluence, full of consumer goods, music, craftmanship, space for human fulfilment. But it is a culture that thrives and is secure only by excluding people. From its profitable markets are driven those who do not conform to the requirements of membership, who do not fully belong and do not support its ideological commitments (13:17). It is a tyrannous community. It is as though the forces with which it is surrounded are slowly creeping in on it, swallowing up its members, focusing their attention more and more on the material wealth and comfort available to them, excluding those who cannot be accommodated. It is as though humanity, driven from the Garden of Eden and excluded from it by the fiery angel, has borrowed some of that fire of judgment to create an alternative Eden, surrounded by it. Inside the ring of fire is perfect bliss and security. But the fire creeps in and closes the circle narrower and narrower.

I do not find it surprising that the community which has protected itself by *these* weapons should have turned into a very ideological community. We tend to think that the Russians are ideological and we are not: that is a great mistake. Since World War II the liberal political philosophies of the West have taken a dramatic turn to liberal ideology. The fruits of this are seen in the tyranny of liberal legislation, which excludes those who are not capable of being totally accommodated to a liberal welfare-community: unwanted children, severely handicapped neonates. It is not surprising that a community which has protected itself with the fire we have protected ourselves with cannot find a place in its markets for those so clearly unfitted for the good life which we propose to lead. And above all, the wretched Third World – not only excluded from our markets, but allowed to become the theatre of our wars which we have carefully banished from *within* the circle of fire. Yes – the forces of chaos have secured us a peace, but what a peace! Those of us who campaign for peace should be terribly careful of what peace we campaign for. The forces of chaos have promised us, and indeed secured us a peace: is it the peace we should want, or is it only that diabolical parody of peace, which stands before God's judgement as violence and wickedness?

Hope and Action

Three visions which illuminate our situation. But what for hope, and what for action?

(1) The prayers of the saints. In Revelation 6:10 the saints cry out 'How long, O Sovereign Lord, how long?' In Revelation 8:3 the incense from the altar, and the prayers of all the saints, let loose the sequence of divine judgement. The first thing we have to understand is good news: humanity, in laying hold of the ultimate forces for our own purposes, in invoking closure on the world for our own ends, never for one moment actually succeeds in seizing the initiative from God. In John's vision it is the prayers of the saints that are in control, because God is in control. Even the very Antichrist himself and *his* kingdom appear at their behest, as they pray for *God's* kingdom, 'Thy kingdom come'! Notice the contrast between the way the saints and the servants of the Antichrist conduct themselves in the face of a common desire. Their desire is for a *final* political peace, an order which will be decisive, which will end all contradiction, which will realise the full possibility of material blessings that creation holds. Moved by this longing the servants of Antichrist seize the apocalyptic powers that will bring such an order about, but the saints pray for God to bring it about, because they know that judgement and new creation lie within His gift and cannot be taken from Him. Their

prayer is a form of renunciation of such power into the hands of Him who inalienably holds it. And *because* they have renounced it, they exercise it more really than those who think they can seize and control it. The saints with their prayers appear to be apolitical: but in fact they are in touch with the springs of that authority which makes all politics possible.

(2) The gathering of the saints. We traced the sequence of seals through to the point at which, under the sixth seal, the kings, generals and politicians invoked upon themselves the ultimate powers of destruction. Like John himself, we waited, and did not proceed immediately to the seventh seal. There is a halt in the apocalypse. The angel cries, 'Do not harm the earth . . . until we have sealed the servants of our God upon their foreheads' (7:3). And then when we reach the seventh seal (8:1) it gives way to 'a silence in heaven for about half an hour'. That silence is the space, the pause in history, which is filled, as chapter 7 has shown us, with the sealing of the saints. That work, the work of the church, takes place in a little space created for it, a space of half-an-hour, in which the hurtling career of humanity to our destruction is held back by God's restraining hand. In this space we can act. We have time – not much, perhaps, but time, real time given to us to be God's agents, to receive and live out that sealing on the forehead in the world. Sufficient time to act for Him and live for Him, sufficient time for us to turn from the panic which seizes us and the hysterical paralysis which this creates, and to act decisively and faithfully in public. There is space for politics, which is, in its essence, public action. The space is still there, as it was when Jeremiah announced to the exiles in Babylon that they had a space of seventy years before the divine intervention, a space in which they should act humanly: plant, marry, build, seek the peace of Babylon and pray for it. Is this 'peace' – Babylonian space in which the Israel is free to act – the same 'peace' of Babylon as falls to its end in Revelation 18? The same and not the same. Babylon is the same, standing and fallen; but in seeking its 'peace' the servant of God does not reinforce and support the continuance of its

false peace, but speaks to it of its true peace. Let us observe
how:

(3) The testimony of the saints. In Revelation 11:3ff. God
appoints two witnesses – they stand for the apostolic testimony of the church, which Jesus sent out two-by-two –
who prophesy in the city. This is their action, to speak the
truth. This is their politics, and God gives to the word of
truth a power which human political life cannot withstand.
'If any one would harm them, fire pours from their mouth
. . . they have power to shut the sky and to turn the waters
into blood' (6). To speak the truth, God's truth, is the course
of political action open to us, and God has promised that it
will be powerful. The witnesses are God's opposition to the
false prophet, the ideologist of the Babylonian civilization,
whose word gives it its idolatrous shape. Their word challenges its shape, calls it to account before God, who is its
peace. What then shall we do? Why, we shall speak the truth,
at all times and in all places, in the Polaris submarine, in the
Ministry of Defence, we shall speak it in the University, in
the Church, in the market place, in the press, and we shall
be armed by it to rip through the web of ideological deceit
which hides us from God's reality. Above all, we shall speak
the truth about ourselves as a world community, confessing
our Babylonian revolt before each other and before God,
'clothed with sackcloth' – that is the work of God's witness.
It is supremely political work, much more really political,
because much more really public, than what is done by the
Antichrist, which is the corruption of politics and
community.

(4) The suffering of the saints. The two witnesses are slain
at last – when their work for God is done, and their death
is the occasion of a great triumph in the city named Sodom
and Egypt and Babylon. Because the deepest mystery of all
in God's plan is that the victory of God's true word will
come about only through the working out of judgement on
our substitute and representative, Jesus Christ, and all His
disciples are called to bear His cross with Him. The authen-
ticity of the true witness is known by its rejection, by its
leading to the cross of Christ, to suffering and to death. In
the end I am not interested in the difference between pacifists,

just war theorists, deterrentists and everything else: they are useful intermediate categories to organize the questions, but in the end there are two kinds of politics, both of them intending peace, both of them involved in conflict. There is the politics that embraces the cross of Christ and the road of suffering as our only way to true peace; and there is the politics that undertakes to conjure up a peace that is guaranteed cross-free. There is plenty of scope for prudence in politics, when it is made the servant of a true witness to the cross of Christ. But when 'prudence' becomes a way of removing the cross from political life, insulating our human peace from the divine means of reconciliation and forgiveness, then it becomes an idolatry. The way of true politics, the way of Babylon's true peace, carries with it the danger of victimization, nay, in the longest run, the certainty of it. I can offer you no way out of that. I can only hold before your eyes the certainty for which John the Seer looked: that the reverse side of Babylon's judgement is the coming of the Son of Man in great glory to reign, and the raising of his faithful witnesses from the dead to come and reign with him in the city whose name is Jerusalem, the mother of us all.

Chris Sugden

'Working with Chris is like having to keep both feet in different worlds,' said the administrator of the Oxford Centre for Mission Studies. 'He is committed to the human aspects of the work – something he learned in India – but I have to keep the place running properly – something one does in Britain.'

Not only does Chris Sugden bring to his work in Britain a Third World perspective, he does so with a healthy and sincere respect for values he gained from his years there. Having worked as the assistant presbyter at St John's Church in Bangalore, he now directs the Oxford Centre which attempts to bring a consciousness about life in the Two-Thirds World to British Christians.

Chris' contribution to this volume reveals two sides of one coin – world hunger and the arms race – but the links he draws go beyond the obvious financial ones.

9: Let Them Eat Bombs

Chris Sugden

World hunger and the arms race are twin challenges to peace which have a deep link between them. Christian peace-making in the context of the arms race and in the context of world hunger requires that we focus on how they are related.

I want at the outset to acknowledge my debt in this material to two Christian leaders, Rene Padilla from Latin America, Coordinator of the Latin American Theological Fraternity, and Vinay Samuel from India, General Secretary of Partnership in Mission Asia. We in the West have a lot to learn from the majority of the world's Christians who live in the Two-Thirds World – Africa, Asia, Latin-America – in situations of poverty, powerlessness and oppression.

Marketing Hunger

The needs of world hunger are spread before us quite regularly by the media, to such an extent that it has become a business to market world hunger, producing money to deal with the problem. It is marketed just like Austin Rover cars, or anything else, by simplifying a situation, taking a very simple aspect of the problem, promoting that, and then getting a response. The trouble with this is that it is a superficial way of dealing with the problem. We need to look not only at the human needs, but beyond those needs to the issues. Behind the issues are the structures, behind those, the groups, and behind the groups, there is a world view.

We start at the level of need in looking at both the arms race and world hunger. Our nation needs security against those who may be potential aggressors. Similarly we can take the need for food, and meet it by providing food.

If we remain at these levels of need we can then link the two issues by saying that we need to make ourselves secure first, then we will feel safe enough to give money to alleviate hunger abroad. We then also need to make two-thirds world feel secure against potential enemies first, and then they will be able to grow enough food. Finally we can try to resolve the issues by saying that we will give money for both defence and food, beginning with our needs first.

Finite Resources

However, that resolution breaks down because the world's resources are finite.

The figures of the Brandt Report are well known:

'More arms do not make mankind safer, only poorer. The world military spending dwarfs any spending on development. Total military expenditures are approaching 450 billion dollars a year, while annual spending on official development aid is only 20 billion dollars. There is a moral link between the vast spending on arms and the disgracefully low spending on measures to remove hunger and ill-health in the Third World. The cost of a ten-year programme to provide for essential food and health needs in developing countries is less than half of one year's military spending. In East and West a very large proportion of scientists and much of scientific resources of universities and industry are devoted to armaments.'[1]

The report shows that it is not possible to make everybody feel secure so that they can have enough to give away or grow enough in their own land. There are not enough

[1]Brandt Report *North South* Pan Books 1980 p. 117–118.

resources to do it and what resources there are, are badly skewed.

Stewardship

Stewardship links together nuclear weapons and world hunger because it calls our attention to what men and women were created to be. We were created to be the image of God and to have dominion over the creation as its managers (Genesis 1:27–28).

The term 'image' is not really expanded in the scriptures because images of God were forbidden. In the ancient Near-East 'image' referred to the representative of the invisible God, most often the statue in the temple, or the king. But we are the managers of creation in the image of God. The image of God for Genesis was not the king, the priest, or a statue. It was everyone together. Our calling to be stewards is the context of our discipleship. In Romans 8:29 Paul says that God's purpose is that we are to be conformed to the image of his Son. Jesus is the true image of God, so we are restored to our true position as managers of creation in Jesus.

This means that discipleship and Christian growth does not only include matters of spiritual discipline or church worship or bible-reading and prayers. Enabling people to manage the resources of the world includes trade, production, and business, making these proper contexts for discipleship as we are being restored into the image of God.

So the first link between world hunger and the nuclear arms race is that both distort our stewardship and prevent other people from being stewards. Everyone is called to be a steward. If someone is prevented from being a steward because they have no access to resources to steward, then their ability to fulfil God's calling to be fully human is stunted. We say, 'Give a man a fish, you feed him for a day; teach him to fish and you feed him for life'; but this is not complete. The question is whether he has access to the fish-ponds. If you prevent people having access to the fish-ponds, access to resources, then they cannot be stewards, what God means them to be. There is a clear link between the nuclear arms race and world hunger; in a world of finite resources they both hinder people's ability to be stewards.

Made or Kept Poor by Others

Behind the fact of hunger is the issue of poverty, oppression and deprivation. For example, India is like Africa twenty years ago, ravaged by a series of famines and droughts. There were massive imports of grain, mostly from the United States, under public law 480 which legislated that certain surplus amounts of grain should be exported at a very cheap price.

Even though India is now self-sufficient in grain, even producing a slight surplus, 60% of the eight hundred million people still live below the poverty line. This is defined by the amount of income needed to buy enough calories to sustain human life at a normal level of functioning. Living below the poverty line does not mean one will starve to death next week. But one would be malnourished and much more vulnerable to disease. One also gets tired much more easily, finds it difficult to maintain a high level of work, and generally gets poorer in a vicious downward spiral. In India, 60% of the population are malnourished and yet India is producing enough food to feed the whole population. The issue is more than lack of resources, people are actually kept poor and dependent.

Groups in Conflict

Behind the arms race is the issue of security and behind the issue of security is the conflict of systems. International capitalism and socialism are directly conflicting systems.

As Christians we believe that the final reality in the universe is relational and that people are the supreme crown of creation. So we must go behind the impersonal structures to groups of people who have made choices which determine what is going on at the moment.

We are told by the scriptures that human choice matters, reaching far into the future, as the sins of the fathers are meted out on the children to the third and fourth generation.

Decisions made three and four generations ago will influence the situation we have now. Human choices can produce a rigid straight jacket in which we are all held. To only blame impersonal structures would be to remain captive to the mechanistic way of thinking about our society: we must have a look at the groups of people.

This is what Jesus did. He identified particular groups of people and their particular group self-interest. For example, he addressed the Pharisees on the whole issue of their distortion of the Jewish law. They had taken the Jewish law out of its context of protecting the poor and weak and preventing injustice in the people of Israel. Rather their focus was their own self-interest, which led finally to making a deal with the Romans.[2]

The Pharisees had remained a powerful group in Israel. To ensure that their understanding of the law would not conflict with Roman colonial rule, they taught that the law was a purely personal and religious requirement that made no statement about politics or any social reality.

Similarly the caste system in India is the group self-interest of the upper castes; the apartheid system in South Africa is also about the self-interest of the ruling white elite. We could say that the international conflict between capitalism and socialism is the group self-interest on the one hand of the capitalist entrepreneurs, and on the other hand the group self-interest of the party which directs the state.

Conflicting World Views

Behind those groups are world views of what human life is all about. Like the Pharisees in Jesus' time or the Brahmins in India, there are always those who provide the ideology for the system created.[3] The world-view of the group lies

[2]See further Vinay Samuel, *The Meaning and Cost of Discipleship*, Paternoster Press 1983 p. 39–47.
[3]This is why inter-faith dialogue is such a crucial issue, because if it is a matter of talking to Brahmins about the spirituality of believing in God they are very happy. But if you talk to them about the social implications of theology, that Jesus was on the side of the poor, and how poor Hindus react to Brahmin theology, it becomes a different matter altogether. Inter-faith dialogue can never be just a matter of discussing religion; it must also include discussions about the ethical, social and political aspects of life.

behind the social structures and issues. The world-view of the Pharisees, who made a compromise with Rome, took the law of Moses out of the context of the Exodus from Egypt and oppression and kept religion separate from society. It was this that Jesus objected to so strongly. He deliberately broke the law to show this on a number of occasions.

The capitalist world-view that the West is based on is world domination through franchising. Any fast food restaurant is a good example of this; they sell someone the franchise, tell them the formula to make their particular recipe, and send them off to sell the product. Those who wear little red and white hats belong, which makes the whole world look like Coca-Cola, destroying any local identity, initiative and self-worth.

Socialism is based on a world view of victory through conflict. It is interesting to remember that Marx was inspired in his ideas by the conflicts in British society. Socialism appears to identify human life in terms of conflict which is inevitably generated by the assumption.

Security and Identity

In all these world-views, security is tied up with the social position of groups in which people find their identity. 'At least we are better than they are.' This attitude is prevalent in the scriptures; the Jews say 'thank goodness we are not like the Gentiles', and the Pharisee says 'Thank God I am not like that tax collector.'

We are still guilty of this today: in Delhi, for example, where the garbage cleaners (a combination of dustmen and gypsies who live off scouring through garbage) call themselves the 'Konjars', the nobodies, because people treat them like dirt. 'They look through us and don't even see us,' they often say. Other people in Delhi gain something of their identity by saying, 'Thank God we are not like them, living off the rubbish.' Our identity is at the expense of another group's sense of self-worth and identity.

The Christian Gospel

How does the Christian Gospel address all these world views? First, while the gospel looks at life at every level, it particularly states that identity and security come through being a child of God by grace.

However, our society is built around work. A recent television programme interviewed a number of people who had become unemployed. One of the interviewees was a former personnel manager whose job it was to cut back on staff and was then sacked himself. 'What does it feel like?' he was asked. 'I felt that I was nothing, I was nobody, I had no role to play, I had no identity.' This is how our society works: our identity is built on our work and our group identity.

The gospel of Jesus Christ tells us who we really are, not how we find identity through a group, or through our work. Identity and security come through being a member of the family of God. The social structure of the Old Testament is based upon the network of families: a group of families making up a clan, and a group of clans making up a tribe.[4] But the basic unit was the family, and in the New Testament this structure is taken up as the model for the life of the church. Paul gives clear instructions that the elders of the church should be good husbands who know how to manage their family well (1 Tim 3:1–5). The term 'elders' is the same as the family in Israelite society. God's work for redemption was through the family and the family of families. This challenges our belief that bigger and better Christian institutions really are the hope for the world.

Secondly, through the gospel, our identity in the family of God, which is given us by grace, transcends conflicting groups. In Ephesians Paul makes it clear that God's purpose is to bring everything into unity with Christ as head: 'The plan which God will complete when the time is right, is to bring all the creation together, everything in heaven and earth, with Christ as head.' (Eph 1:10). That plan has already been achieved by the cross of Christ. In Ephesians 3:9–10 Paul writes,

[4]See Christopher J. H. Wright 'The Ethical Relevance of Israel as a Society' in *Transformation* Vol. 1 No. 4 October 1984.

'God gave me the privilege of making all people see how God's secret plan of uniting everything together with Christ as head is being put into effect. God who is the creator of all things kept his secret hidden through all the past ages, in order that, at the present time, by means of the church the angelic rulers and powers in the heavenly world might learn of his wisdom in all its different forms.'

The plan is being put into operation by the church. What is the church? It is a group of people who transcend conflicting groups. The 'secret' is that by means of the gospel, the Gentiles have a part with the Jews in God's blessing. Ephesians 3:6: 'They are members of the same body and share in the promise that God made through Christ Jesus.' The church has Jews and Gentiles together in one body to demonstrate God's wisdom to the angelic rulers and powers in the heavenly world – the principalities and powers whose focus is to create division, and set people against each other. The church is the sign that their power is broken.

Paul made this a very crucial issue in his letter to the Roman Church. They had started to get involved in a sort of 'house church movement'. There were house church groups made up of Jewish Christians who would not have fellowship with Gentile Christians, or only very occasionally, and house church groups of Gentile Christians who would not have any fellowship with Jewish Christians, and others who would occasionally meet with Jewish Christians. The Gentile Christians called themselves 'strong in the faith', and identified the Jewish Christians as 'weak'. Another example of ones identity at the expense of another's.

These conflicting groups needed to accept one another as Christ accepted them (Romans 15:7). Gentile Christians need to remember that the father of faith, Abraham, was a Jew. Jewish Christians who prized Moses, Abraham and the law needed to remember that these can never be a requirement for becoming a Christian. Salvation is by faith, Abraham was called by God through faith and was saved through faith. Christians, Paul writes, should accept one another as Christ has accepted them: by faith. The good news that Paul declares is that the gospel has already broken down the divisions and conflicts and that by grace people can be in one body through Christ. The coming of the Kingdom of God through the death and resurrection of Jesus, creating a church made up of people from different cultures in one body, is the way that right relationships and justice are established.

This is what Christian social action is all about. It is not about trying to formulate a perfect set of laws so that if only the government would put them into action we would have a more Christian society. Nor is it about forming lobby groups in order to press one point of view or another, although that may be part of the work to which we are called. The church is called to social involvement by its very being. The task of the whole church is to proclaim and demonstrate that Jesus Christ is God's way of establishing right relationships in his family of families. The church's role is to demonstrate how God establishes justice, how God establishes right relationships by giving people a new identity through Christ, bringing together people of different cultural backgrounds in the family of families thus strengthening the family as the unit of society which God has ordained for its redemption. This is not a special duty for people concerned about peace; this is at the heart of what it means to be committed to Jesus Christ and saved by him.

Conflict or Co-operation

Thirdly, the gospel tells us that disorder in human relationships is not settled by strife. The conflict model and theory says that in human society you have got to settle things by strength and conflict. This was the Romans' view of society. But Jesus said,

'You know that the men who are considered rulers of the heathen have complete power over them, and the leaders have complete authority. However, this is not the way it is among you; if one of you wants to be great he must be the servant of the rest.' (Mark 10:42–43).

Jesus doesn't want us to play the power game.

There was a peace conference about three years ago in Uppsala, Sweden, which was the largest gathering of representatives from Christian denominations that the world has ever seen. The recently assassinated Prime Minister of Sweden, Olav Palme, put forward the idea that the whole nuclear issue is encompassed by the question of whether you think that human society best solves its problems by conflict or co-operation. Where we stand as Christians on this issue is crucial.

Maintaining Peace

Fourthly, the gospel tells us that peace is not maintained by 'mutually assured destruction'. Christians who do not come from white societies tell us that mutually assured destruction between white races, as a means of keeping world peace is racism. John Perkins, a black Christian in the U.S., posed the question, 'What would we feel if it was Khomeni and Gaddafy who were standing against each other with these arsenals that were supposed to ensure the peace?' Would we feel quite so secure? It is our tribe who hold the arsenals, and that is why we think we are secure. This is racist.

The Christian gospel says that peace is maintained by justice. The prophet Isaiah wrote, 'Because everyone will do what is right there will be peace and security for ever. The fruit of justice will be peace; the effect of justice will be quietness and security for ever.' (Isaiah 32:17) Rene Padilla, a pastor from Buenos Aires, writes:

'Injustice is the order of the day, yet injustice does not come alone. Where justice is disregarded, anarchy breaks in . . . . Law and order used as rationalizations to justify the oppressors inevitably lose all respect from the oppressed, the victims of the system which invokes them. Ethical values are then increasingly ignored. The situation which emerges is that which the prophet suggests when he says "Woe to those who call evil good and good evil, who put darkness for light and light for darkness, who put bitter for sweet and sweet for bitter." (Isaiah 5:20) All sense of right and wrong is lost and social chaos takes over.'[5]

When justice is ignored, peace is lost. Isaiah makes a clear link between justice and peace in chapter 32:17–19: 'God's people will be free from worries and their homes peaceful and safe. How happy everyone will be with plenty of water for the crops and safe pasture everywhere for the donkeys and cattle.' Isaiah is reminding the people that in the law of Moses it was clear that if they obeyed God's commandments there would be peace, but if they disobeyed God there would be all sorts of chaos and disorder.

In the absence of justice only a counterfeit peace is possible. Padilla writes:

'The only peace possible in a society which neglects justice is the peace imposed by national security regimes. A peace totally dependent on persecution and exile, arbitrary arrest and torture, forced disappearances, mutilations and assassinations. A peace built on bloodshed, a sham peace, especially designed for a wealthy privileged elite, but bought with the lives of the oppressed. A false peace, for the poor abhor it and the rich cannot fully enjoy it; a peace that threatens to blow up modern civilization.'[6]

Identity at no-one's expense

The Christian gospel tells us that fundamentally people's identity and security both as individuals and groups are critical to peace. How then can people gain their true identity without it being at the expense of others?

Jesus would tell us that we become the people of God, through grace and allegiance to him, identifying status as a key issue. If the Old Testament focuses on economics for obedience, the New Testament focuses on status.[7] John the

[5]Rene Padilla 'The Fruit of Justice will be Peace' in *Transformation* Vol. 2 No. 1 p. 2.
[6]Padilla op. cit. p. 3.
[7]See Stephen Mott *Jesus and Social Ethics* Grove Booklets 1985, and also 'The Use of the New Testament in Social Ethics' in *Transformation* Vol. 1 Nos. 3 & 4 July and October 1984.

Baptist spoke to people who were very proud of being Jews, and said that God would turn the stones into children of Abraham. Men were very proud of their status, but Jesus gave equal status to women. He took a child and said 'Whoever receives one of these receives me and whoever receives me receives the one who sent me.' He put a child on an equal with him, as a bearer of the presence of God – treating children as children, not as tomorrow's adults. The whole work and mission of the church was to bring the outcasts into the family of God. Jesus taught that genuine status was simply the gift of God through grace, creating a new self-identity and a new freedom to be servants without having to find status through position or strength.

How do we empower people to discover their true identity? Not through the superiority of their group, nor the success of an individual. In this country we are not obsessed as much with large group solidarity, but with individual success. But as Christians we are not to find our identity in that sort of way. We are to find our identity as a child of God through grace and as a member of the family of God; we are called to be stewards and to manage the resources he has given us. Therefore we are to enable other people to have access to resources and to control resources – not for their own individual benefit, but as servants for the benefit of the whole community.

The Christian response to the arms race and world hunger must be an acknowledgement of the fundamental problem they represent. It is not enough to make people feel guilty or fearful, or to form another crusade – the benefits produced by this will burn out in ten years. We are to free people to enable them to discover their true identity, to understand how they are being oppressed and alienated, to make them aware of the forces that are robbing them of true identity, and then to become agents of the gospel of the power of God. Then they can enable others to be released from this alienating situation and to be true servants.

The linking of hunger and the arms race is not a matter of taking two single issues and saying there is a financial link between them. The question is whether when someone's God-given identity is being distorted or obliterated, are we able to point it out and say, 'This is not God's will for human life'? We must enable people to be truly human and remember this as a gift of grace.

The War is Over – Celebrate the Peace

There is a story that, at the end of World War II, allied prisoners from Poland and North America in a prisoner-of-war camp were receiving news from a secret radio. They were able to communicate the news to other groups of prisoners separated by wire fences because the chaplains were able to speak to each other once a day in a common language. When the news came through that the Germans had surrendered, the chaplains passed the news to the other chaplains through the wire. But the German guards had not heard the news, so they could not understand why the prisoners were suddenly walking around smiling and talking. The war was over and the victory had been won, even though the fences and the guards remained.

That is a picture of where we are: the war is over, evil has been defeated; Christ has won and victory has been established. The work of the church is to announce to people that they are free, and to enable them to enjoy their freedom, whether through fair trade, or international relations that are not built on conflict. The strong man has been bound – we are in the business of freeing people. That freedom must be expressed, experienced, and encouraged in the everyday realities of food and harmony as people are enabled to be stewards of God's world together.

Sue Conlan

There is a new generation of evangelical women in Britain who, in coming to know themselves more deeply as full persons before God, have broadened their struggle to embrace other causes for justice. Sue Conlan is one such woman. Her ministry has come to be associated with work for justice among black people in this country. It is not a work separate from her feminist commitments, nor from her efforts for peace, as will be recognized in this chapter, 'Racism and the Bomb'.

In the following pages, Sue helps us to break down divides between the evil institutions of racism and of the nuclear arms industry. By so doing, she uncovers the quest for power which keeps black people, and now white as well, at the mercy of the powerful few who hold not only wealth and political control over us, but now also the nuclear key.

10: Racism and the Bomb

Sue Conlan

It is often thought that racism and nuclear weapons have little in common. For many white Christians, racism is an unpleasant fact of life which few would endorse. Similarly, the reality of nuclear weapons, with their ever present threat to life, leads many to agree that some form of reduction is necessary. But rarely do we go beyond our armchair concern to actively link the movements of justice and peace, even though it could be argued that combatting nuclear weapons is a luxury that most people of the world cannot afford. Theirs is a daily struggle for survival.

But the link was made most poignantly for me when I was walking through a women's peace camp at Greenham Common. There stood a statue of a woman, a pregnant woman carved out of brown stone and hanging upon a cross. And this brown woman spoke a silent message to all who could hear: 'Here I hang, my child and I, crucified in the name of your peace'. That realization is not easy to live with. Yet from Hiroshima and Nagasaki onwards, a nuclear holocaust has been inflicted by East and West upon the populations of Africa and Asia. And when we come nearer to home, the doctrine of 'national security' has been used to justify the denial of freedom to black people.

Just before beginning work in January 1982 with an organization which was then called the Evangelical Race Relations Group (ERRG), I had seen a little of the reality of black people's lives in Britain by being involved, for example, in trying to counter the racism of Britain's immigration laws.

Those laws in themselves fly in the face of an acceptable understanding of the freedom that is meant to accompany peace in Britain. But it was not until working with ERRG that I linked up the anti-nuclear movement with anti-racism.

Having been something of an 'activist' before being appointed Field Worker with ERRG, I then found myself in an ivory tower, removed from the people on whose behalf I was meant to be working, learning theories about racism from books and passing on my knowledge to other white, middle class 'professionals'. Any sense of the struggle that was developing in my own commitment was in danger of being anaesthetized. But the feeling of needing to be closer to the ground was shared by members of the ERRG Committee, and the organization moved office from Nottingham city centre to the edge of a council estate in Birmingham in December 1983.

As the organization set itself on the way to a closer identification with the struggles that black people face in Britain, and indeed more attentive to the voice of those black people involved with the work, so its perspective has become more international and its links become closer with other movements for justice and peace.

Two worlds – black and white

While at college, I joined the World Development Movement out of a concern for the gap between the 'rich North' and the 'poor South'. I even waded through the heavy content of the Brandt Report which was published at the same time! But having learnt history from a white British perspective, it never really dawned at that time that what I was looking at was essentially a divide between the white North and the black South.

I gained a more accurate understanding of history when I learnt it from the 'underside' – from the experience of those who were ruled by the British Empire. It was then that I began to realize just how much I had been lied to and that the process of un-learning white history demanded much more than a change of attitude and good personal relationships. After all, if British society is built upon injustice and oppression, it's not going to go away if I'm nice to my black neighbour! The exploitation of black people's lives, land and resources is still widespread and our 'peace' is bought at their expense. As Barbara Rogers writes:

> The economic and political practices, including the race for resources, arising out of the strategic and military competition between the super-powers – the United States and the Soviet Union and their allies – are also instrumental in perpetuating this pattern of worldwide domination. . . . Among the values on which the (world) system is based are self-interest and greed which seek to dominate and exploit the people and resources of the world and use them for the benefit of the few. This system is racist in a variety of ways: it sets the framework for world order based on the values and interests of the white world; it was historically based on the exploitation of peoples of colour, and it projects a continued and expanding exploitation of their land and resources.[1]

The link between global racism and nuclear weapons is perhaps best understood in terms of what the world most values. As President Eisenhower said:

> Every gun that is made, every warship that is launched, every rocket fired signifies a theft from those that hunger and are not fed, from those that are cold and are not clothed.[2]

Hence campaigns with slogans such as 'disarm for development' and 'bread not bombs'. But it is obviously easier to turn swords into ploughshares in our statements than to make it real in political practice. Even the limited 'aid' or 'development' that does take place from the white world to the two-thirds World, has purse strings attached to the interests of the rich. A new order requires much more than 'disarm for development' may suggest. It necessitates a complete re-structuring in the interests of the poor. For

[1]Barbara Rogers: *Race – No Peace Without Justice* (pp. 78, 105) WCC 1980
[2]Address entitled 'The Chance for Peace' (April 1953).

behind nuclear weapons lies the white world's self-acclaimed right to dominate and destroy fellow members of the human race.

Peace in our time?

Although many of the native countries of black people are now free from direct European colonisation, the effect of a world-system ordered in the interests of white people lingers on. In 1947, the United Nations granted the Marshall Islands in the Pacific, land inhabited by Aborigines, to the United States government to administrate as a Trust Territory. In March 1954, the US, carrying out nuclear tests in the area, dropped a 15 metagon hydrogen bomb, the radioactive fall-out being blown over the islands of Rongelapland Utirik. Etry Enos, a Rongelap woman, reported:

When we moved to Majuro (three days after the bomb was dropped), we continued to have sickness. Many forms of miscarriage and still-birth occurred. My older sister had a baby like a crab and another woman had a baby without a skull. Some women gave birth to creatures like cats, rats, and the inside of turtles – maybe like intestines. Some women even stopped having children, including me.[3]

The Aborigine people have been accustomed to forcible removal from their lands upon being 'discovered' by white travellers many years previously. This time they were not removed because they were useful as guinea pigs to see what the effect of the nuclear bomb would be. As colonial exploitation was justified by considering black people as animals, the same pattern returns in a different guise.

During the General Election of June 1983, I spent some time canvassing on behalf of the Labour Party, whose manifesto included a commitment to nuclear disarmament. Some of the traditional Labour supporters I met had been convinced by one of the most common arguments used in

[3]Quoted in Dawn Glazier: The Struggle for Survival in the Pacific (Peace News).

favour of nuclear weapons, namely that they have kept the peace for forty years.

Much has been written about the biblical understanding of peace, particularly the Hebrew word 'shalom', and how different its meaning is from the absence of war. The disturbances that took place in British cities in 1981 and 1985, when black and white young people together expressed their anger against a system which uses and abuses them, demonstrate the lack of real peace in Britain.

But even ignoring what happens on 'British soil', including Northern Ireland, it is estimated that over 30 million people have died in wars fought with conventional weapons since 1945. The reason we are led to believe that this is a peaceful situation is that most of the victims have been black – people of the two-thirds World. Yet most of the weapons have been made in the factories of Europe and North America and supplied through an arms trade whose aim is profit, not peace. The ongoing battle between East and West over the resources of the Third World, increases the possibility of war in the territories of Europe and North America.

Apartheid and the Trident programme

As part of the political and military competition between East and West, Britain has been involved in helping to maintain the most racist regime in the world. With its claim to be a 'Christian nation', South Africa stands in opposition to faith in God, who is with the poor and the oppressed. It remains the stronghold of white minority domination, kept secure by the financial and military support of other capitalist powers. The regime itself possesses nuclear weapons, some of which are believed to be sited in Namibia, a country it occupies illegally, despite the demands of the Namibian people for liberation. With Britain's refusal to make its condemnation of apartheid any stronger than empty words, the racist philosophy of South Africa gets Britain's assent in the defence of white domination.

The strongest link between racism and nuclear proliferation is the uranium mining activities of British-based Rio

Tinto Zinc (RTZ) in Namibia. RTZ is the largest mining corporation in the world and the sixth largest company in Britain. Its operations in Namibia are in direct contravention of the United Nations Decree No. 1 (for the Protection of the Natural Resources of Namibia), which states:

No person or entity . . . may search for, prospect for, explore for, take, extract, mine, process, refine, use, sell, export or distribute any natural resource, whether animal or mineral, situated or found to be situated within the territorial limits of Namibia.

In November 1982, Tony Benn (Secretary of State for Energy from 1975 to 1979), gave evidence to the Commission of Inquiry set up to investigate legal aspects of RTZ's mining operations in South Africa. In his evidence he stated his belief that the demand for uranium in Britain had begun with the build-up of weapons after the Second World War, and continues today unabated. It has been estimated that the Ministry of Defence will need 2,000 tonnes of uranium oxide by the end of this decade to provide fuel and warheads for the Trident programme, the U.S.-produced nuclear submarine system. Other producers of uranium, such as Canada, only make supply available if there is a guarantee that it is not used in a nuclear weapons programme. South Africa has no such requirement and the Anti-Apartheid Movement has estimated that 60% of British uranium is supplied from RTZ's Rossing Mine in Namibia, some of which will be used in the Trident programme. A leaflet produced by the Campaign Against Namibian Uranium Contracts states:

If strategic missiles for their first strike weapons system are secure, the British government is content to watch the war in Namibia drag on.

In other words, if racial oppression is an aid to the economic, political or military aspirations of government and industry, then it will be actively encouraged or conveniently ignored.

RTZ's mining operations in Namibia, and Britain's support through both its civil and military nuclear programmes, have at least two effects upon the black people of Namibia: they divide families and communities in a desire to exploit black labour but not to be otherwise associated with black people; the conditions in the mines and living quarters of the miners, and those of their families in the 'homelands' or reserves, lead to poor health, disease and slow or premature death.

Namibia, like South Africa, operates a migrant labour system whereby the men provide their labour on a contract basis, away from their homes and families for lengthy periods (for example, 12 to 18 months). RTZ's Rossing Mine is the largest open-cast mine in the world. The black miners receive one-tenth of the pay of white miners (whose ranks were increased by an influx of white people upon the independence of Zimbabwe). No attempt has been made to monitor the level of radiation to which the miners are exposed. The dangers of this are expressed in a letter written by a workers' representative at Rossing Mine:

Working in the open air under the hot sun, in the uranium dust produced by the grinding machines, we are also exposed to the ever present cyclonic wind which is blowing in the desert. Consequently, our bodies are covered in dust and one can hardly recognize us. We are inhaling the uranium dust into our lungs so that many of us have already suffered an effect.[4]

And from a representative of the South West African People's Organization:

The biggest problem is contamination from uranium. When the men return to the reserves they pass on the contamination. Diseases such as tuberculosis spread and speculation has it that men can often become impotent. One paper referred to Namibia as 'the land of the sterile women' because of the alleged effects of contamination

[4]Extract from a Workers' Representatives letter at Rossing Mine.

on fertility. There are few health clinics or hospitals and treatment costs money. So the women bear the burden of looking after the sick, are forced to walk for days and weeks in search of the few doctors available. Lack of money and food means that the children die of malnutrition.[5]

On the fortieth anniversary of the bombs dropped at Hiroshima and Nagasaki, British television programmes portrayed the possible effects of a nuclear attack upon Britain. Having been brought up with a belief in life after death, perhaps I should not have been disturbed. But the cries of many for life *before* death is a much more demanding belief that requires, at the very least, the removal of nuclear weapons from the face of God's earth.

White nation

While Britain's interests lie with the white powerful world, its attitudes and policies towards black people will continue to be racist. That means that racism can never be limited to Britain's relations with other nations, but comes right back home to how black people are treated in Britain.

ERRG changed its name to Evangelical Christians for Racial Justice (ECRJ) in January 1985. In the same month we held our Annual Conference on the theme of racism and nationalism. Rev. Ken Leech,[6] in a talk under the title of 'The Politics of Nationhood', reflected upon the consequences of the Falklands Campaign for nationalism in Britain. Mrs. Thatcher, in her victory speech on 3rd July 1982, declared that the campaign had undermined the belief that

Britain was no longer a nation that had built an Empire and ruled a quarter of the world. Well, they were wrong. The lesson of the Falklands is that Britain has not changed.

Ken Leech remarked:

[5]Pendukeni Kaulinge, South West African People's Organization, Secretary for Women.
[6]Race Relations Field Officer, Church of England Board for Social Responsibility.

We need to ask: where are Black British people in this thinking? For Black people did not rule a quarter of the world: they were ruled *by* the Empire.[7]

But Mrs. Thatcher is not alone in suffering from 'Empire mentality'. The whole pro-nuclear lobby keeps her company.

The purpose of the East-West confrontation over nuclear capability is to instil fear into 'the enemy' so that they will not commit the crime of genocide. In the name of 'national security', British people have been bombarded with the idea that Communist Russia is looking for an opportunity to take over our nation of freedom and democracy. Ken Leech also made the point that black people are excluded from most white people's definitions of the British 'nation'. The same doctrine of national security which polices communism has been used to treat black British people as an internal threat to stability. A World Council of Churches working group on 'Racism and National Security Systems' reported:

> Security is achieved by ensuring to all people economic, political, social, and cultural justice and their full participation in the life of the nation.[8]

But along with Britain's nuclear policy, a heavy-handed approach to 'law and order' also contravenes such a biblical principle. Legislation and administrative measures have been passed by parliament to control black people and to limit their freedom (for example, the Police and Criminal Evidence Act 1984 and Immigration Rules). At a meeting of the Monday Club at the Conservative Party Conference in October 1982, Inspector Basil Griffiths, deputy Chairman of the Police Federation, said:

> There is in our inner cities a very large minority of people who are not fit for salvage. . . . The only way the police can protect society is quite simply by harassing those

---

[7]Ken Leech: *The Politics of Nationhood*. Available from ECRJ for 10p. (plus p&p.)
[8]Quoted in Barbara Rogers: *Race – No Peace Without Justice* (p. 109).

people and frightening them so they are afraid to commit crime.[9]

Violence is often portrayed as the monopoly of the 'terrorist' or the criminal. Rarely is the word applied to governments, even when they themselves adopt the characteristics of the terrorist. So we hear little about the 'structural violence' of a society which denies black and white working class people the same access to jobs, housing, education and health care, as their white middle and upper class contemporaries enjoy. While 'defence' is paid for daily by black people abroad, the treatment of those at the bottom of British society presents the question: What is it we're defending? For like the black welfare mothers of Mississippi, who refused to send their sons to fight in Vietnam while their own needs were ignored, the 'defence' of Britain is not for the benefit of the majority, but for those few who have the wealth and power to enjoy an unjust structure. The only difference a nuclear war presents is that it is also a threat for those who could buy their security in a conventional war.

Racism – no peace without justice

Racism and nuclear weapons present white people with a choice. Whereas we might come to the anti-nuclear movement out of a concern that Hiroshima may be visited upon us, we must learn that the bomb is being paid for now by black people worldwide. So our choice is between white supremacy and black survival; between 'national security' and the demand of black people to live in freedom and peace; between international pride and the black struggle for self-determination and independence.

That choice has to be made in the light of the lessons that these situations have taught – that struggles for justice and peace are inseparable. The hope for a peaceful future lies just as much with the resistance of black people fighting for their liberation and survival, as it does with any anti-nuclear movement. As Fannie Lou Hamer, a black woman active in

[9]Reported in *The Times* (7.10.1982)

the civil rights movement in America, said: 'The freedom of the white woman is shackled in chains to mine, and she is not free until I am free.'

As a middle class white woman, my freedom lies in the liberation of the world's exploited peoples from their sentence to slow or sudden death. The priorities of our movements should reflect that dependency and be determined by those who suffer most, those who Jesus calls his sisters and brothers when he said: 'Whatever you did not do for one of the least of these, you did not do for me.'

What God made explicit in the incarnation is that he is found amongst the poor and the oppressed. The divinity of God was placed into the vulnerability of human pregnancy, dependent for life upon a woman and her well-being. Would we stand by and allow Mary, the mother of Jesus, to suffer malnutrition under apartheid, or live amidst radioactive fall-out in the Pacific, or suffer sudden nuclear death at Hiroshima? The brown woman at Greenham answers for us: God who was crucified 2,000 years ago by religious arrogance and military oppression, is to be found today amongst the crucified peoples of the world.

Sue Conlan worked with Evangelical Christians for Racial Justice until December 1985. The writing of this article was assisted by Paul Grant and Mark Haman.

Author's Note: 'Black' is used in a political sense, and refers to all non-white people who have suffered and resisted the racism of colonial exploitation and its more recent forms.

Phil Mitchell

It was in the spring of 1981 that Phil Mitchell first expressed publicly his opposition to nuclear weapons. But he took his stance not to the streets, nor to Parliament, but to the evangelical organization for which he works: Frontier Youth Trust. He found, as do many, that often the most difficult tasks of peacemaking are to be found close to home: in the workplace or church, among family or friends.

His convictions have only grown stronger since that time. As FYT staff member for the Northwest, he works to develop outreach to the young and disenfranchised, often victimized by political and economic forces. In this chapter, Phil goes beyond those immediate sources of oppression to the bomb and writes passionately of the connections which exist.

11: Theft from the Poor

Phil Mitchell

'The cry of the poor is the voice of God in agony in our midst'[1]. So wrote Bishop Colin Winter shortly before his death in 1981. The modern world is an urban world. In England over 80% of the population lives in towns and cities. The whole of the western world is urbanized in its mode of life, even if a minority still inhabit the countryside. There is also unprecedented growth in the developing countries creating radical social and economic changes within them. Cities of over 5,000,000 will increase from 29 today to 58 by the end of the century. The twin factors of rapid urbanization and exploding population growth are combining to produce, by the year 2000, the problems of alienated youth on a gigantic scale. For instance Mexico City, with a population projected to turn 31,000,000 by 2000 AD, is expected to have 7,000,000 young unemployed on its hands. Thus we are likely to see the problems of alienated young people in our cities on an unprecedented scale, with crime, prostitution, homelessness, family breakup, drug and alcohol abuse, and violence escalating.

The cry for peace and justice around the world is the voice of God yearning for wholeness for His creation. We hear the sob of God from Ethiopia in the midst of cruel suffering, from South Africa as the voiceless claim a voice, behind the door of the prison cell in the Soviet Union, from the torture chambers of Central and South America, from the youngster

[1]Bishop Colin Winter, *The Burden of Prophesy* S.C.M.

hooked on drugs in some deserted corner of our own inner cities, from the homeless poor and hungry in the United States, the richest nation on earth. The cry goes up and in that cry we can hear the sob of God over His broken world.

Biblically peace and justice are inextricably bound together, the restoration of all things is the goal of the Kingdom of God. 'Through death and resurrection of his Son, God's grace has provided his way to reclamation and reconstitution of the universe. Every unresponsive thing, structure and person will be eradicated; injustice, greed, disease, hunger – all that makes for death and finally death itself will be destroyed. Then the new creation, in "new heavens and new earth" will manifest freely the *Kingdom of God*' (Rev 21:1–5; Is 65:17; Rom 8:21; Is 11:6–9). The Kingdom of God is the Kingdom of the future. Through the Spirit of God we have now the presence of the future and the means of experiencing the realities of the Kingdom for whose coming we pray.[2]

We need to explore the connection between the ever-increasing burden of arms expenditure and the ever-increasing miseries of the poor.

The Lütheran Bishops in the U.S.A. have said,

'The nation's fundamental priorities are reflected in the budget choices it makes. . . . Amid the clamour of various groups seeking to protect their own interests the Church must speak clearly on behalf of those at home and abroad whose pressing human needs require not only private charity but also government action. . . . The sacrifice required must be distributed in accordance with the ability of individual and groups to bear it. The allocation of limited resources should be based on a thorough evaluation of the utility and effectiveness of tax breaks, military spending and social programmes. Given the rate of both unemployment and poverty, we believe that a top budget priority should be securing adequate funding for human needs and income maintenance programmes. No one should be forced to go hungry or homeless or lack adequate medical care'.[3]

[2]Jim Punton – Community for the King: Frontier Youth Trust.
[3]American Lutheran Bishops Report.

But many are so forced. Cut backs in welfare spending, housing programmes, support for voluntary agencies has meant many more being forced to live below the poverty line, feeling trapped and hopeless in living conditions described even by government ministers as 'intolerable'[4].

Our inner cities are the result of historic exploitation. They are our own 'homelands', generated by systemic policies of economic and social discrimination within the multi-cultural complexity of post-industrial Britain. They are not an accident; they are the inevitable result of these policies.

If budget choices are a clear demonstration of a nation's priorities, we must ask what the Christian response is to be to those trapped in high rise tenements on desolate housing estates; to the young unemployed hanging around job centres and city centres; or pensioners facing hunger and hypothermia; the 4,000,000 unemployed; the single parent, and overcrowded prisons. Unemployed young people being forced to move from one place to another in search not only of work, but a place to live, thus creating a new class of 'nomad' young people designated as 'social security scroungers' not fit to look for work in the 'nicer' parts of the country. All this is in direct conflict with the 'upside down' values of the Kingdom of God. This is institutionalized injustice masquerading as a policy of economic recovery. Such policies are morally and spiritually bankrupt when seen in the light of Kingdom values. Can we see, hear and feel the agony of God in this?

Only as we see Jesus in the faces of the poor, and hear the words, 'inasmuch as you did it not to the least of these *my brethren*, you did it not to me', will we truly see and feel the agony of God.

It is this same agony we hear as we face the idolatry of the nuclear arms race. Essentially, the arms race is theft from the poor, in the name of national security. We see the price being paid for our nuclear arsenals in the wasted bodies and frustrated hopes of the world's poor, in the decaying inner cities and deteriorating services in our own country.

Resources already unequally available are further distorted

[4]Michael Heseltine M.P. Liverpool 1982.

by the ever-increasing cost of maintaining, 'our own independent nuclear deterrent'. Clearly it is not 'our own', nor
is it 'independent'; there is no possible scenario where we
independently could use it apart from a final act of naked
vengeance.

Justice and Peace

Justice and peace are seen together supremely in the
awesome agony of Calvary. The place where, 'Heaven's love
and heaven's justice meet'. The cross of Christ is the great
teacher of peace through justice. Jesus was 'making peace
through the blood of the cross'. The cross is the supreme
example of this truth.

The dark hill outside Jerusalem was the greatest demonstration that in the heart and mind of God justice and peace
cannot be separated. What His justice demanded, His love
provided for. Christians' stand for justice and our work for
peace, are based on the revealed character of God. Those
who follow Him are called to be peacemakers: 'Happy are
those who work for peace' (Matt 5:9).

Jim Punton writes:

. . . the Christ Community must see itself as an agent for
the elimination of the structural injustices arising from
race, class, privilege and power. There is no shalom (peace
– wholeness) where excess and bitter poverty co-exist in
neighbourhood or nation, where high production is at the
expense of wasted nature and quality of life, where the
wealth of one group or country is at the expense of others,
where expenditure on armaments obscenely outweighs
relief suffering, where persons are manipulated and made
subservient to technology and bureaucracy, where
freedom is declared by regimes whose prisons reek of
oppression and injustice. As Jesus ranges Himself against
all that prevents and destroys man's shalom, so must His
Body, its feet shod in readiness to speed with good news
of Shalom (Eph 6:15).[5]

[5]*God's Radical Alternative*, Frontier Youth Trust.

By definition the Christian peacemaker is an activist. We are to be makers of peace, but many Christians understand this almost entirely in personal terms. Rather we are called to be activists in what makes for shalom, the full orbed wholeness and peace willed by God for the whole creation. This shows how far we have come away from our roots in historic Judaism and have allowed Greek and Roman ideas of peace to inform our understanding of what the Bible is saying. The Greek idea of peace was largely the absence of conflict or hostility; the Romans enforced peace by the might of arms. The Christian peacemaker is an activist – a creator of peace – and peacemakers are those who contribute actively, joyfully and hopefully to the full manifestation of the peace and justice which is a sign of the kingdom among us now. Peacemakers are God's activists engaged in the task of healing in a broken world.

Justice and peace bring the First and Third worlds together. The Third World's cry for justice is echoed by the First World's cry for peace. This is all the more poignant when we realize that the injustice experienced by the world's poor is directly related to the policy of 'peace through strength' which in reality means the illusion of peace by robbing the poor of what is rightly theirs. The increasing world wide urbanization now taking place is creating conditions where scarce resources are unable to support those flocking to the cities. From the shanty towns of South America, the Toxteths of Britain, the bustees of India, the ghettos of the USA and the slums of Australia the cry is heard.

'People are coming to see that the way of Jesus is the way of Peace. Those who preach fear, prejudice, hysteria, and hatred are simply not preaching the gospel of Jesus. It is spiritually and politically disastrous to try to separate the struggle for justice from the relentless pursuit of peace. You have only to be in a place where the poor are already bearing the consequences of a war economy to see that connection. It is even deeper on a spiritual level. The Bible does not make those distinctions. The biblical vision is one of shalom – justice and peace and well-being and healing and wholeness – where health and justice of the whole community is encompassed in that biblical vision of justice and peace'.[6]

The mechanisms which make and keep people poor are those same mechanisms, which in the name of national security, not only increase insecurity, but increase the dependency and misery of the poor.

President Eisenhower once said, 'Every gun that is made, every warship launched every rocket fired, signifies in a final sense a theft from those who hunger and are not fed, from those who are cold and not clothed.'

The arms race is theft from the poor in the name of national security. Arms expenditure is not a forced choice, it is a deliberate choice, to which we contribute via taxation. Those who give money to alleviate the hunger of Ethiopia also 'give' money to the government via taxation to increase the arms race beyond anything necessary, thus at the same time compounding the miseries of the poor.

Industrial Conversion

Conversion to a non-nuclear defence will include the conversion of the arms industry. There are no simplistic answers to this and we need great sensitivity when approaching those engaged in the arms industries. In an era of high unemployment the last thing people want are well meaning peace people threatening their jobs and well-being, quite possibly from their own position of secure employment.

President Jimmy Carter said in 1976,

It is easier to talk about beating 'swords into ploughshares', than it is to convert a production line from jet fighters to subway cars . . . we must face the reality that millions of Americans depend on military spending for their economic livelihood . . . we must face these prob-

6Jim Wallis from an interview in 'City Cries', *Journal of Evangelical Coalition for Urban Mission.*

lems squarely through intelligent and long range conversion planning. . . .[7]

But workers in the arms industries have been faced with a false choice. They have been told that spending on weapons creates jobs, and if the military budget is reduced their jobs will be put at risk.

There is now substantial evidence that the reverse is true, and that the heavy burden placed on the economy by years of high arms spending generally undermines the economy. In 1976 the US Bureau of Labour Statistics estimated that for every one million dollars spent, 75,000 jobs would be created in defence, as against 100,000 in construction, 112,000 in consumer goods, 138,000 in health and 187,000 in education.

Britain spends more of its Gross National Product (£8,000,000,000 per year which is the measure of the total goods and services produced by the economy and taking into account inward and outward investment) on defence than any of its European allies; 5.3%, at the present. It has been estimated this could rise to 7.2% by the end of the 1980s.

The Ministry of Defence is one of the country's largest employers. Well over 1,000,000 people are employed as a result of defence spending. There are more than 60 contractors with whom the Ministry of Defence places more than £5 million worth of business every year, and at any one time it has contracts with over 10,000 companies. Defence accounts for almost half the output of the British aerospace industry and one third of the output of the British electronics industry. Over half of Britain's research and development is devoted to military purposes. The arms industry has an insatiable appetite.

The British arms industry is clearly very big business. What this means is that at a time when scientific and technological potential has never been greater, this country is failing to harness that potential to useful production. Those indus-

[7]Taken from a statement during the election campaign, September 18, 1976, as quoted by Seymour Melman, 'Beating Swords into Subways', *The New York Times Magazine*, November 12, 1978.

tries expected to play a major role over the next two decades at least – tele-communications, robotics, biotechnology – need a lot of research and development prior to production. This cannot be done when 54% of this is devoted to armaments.

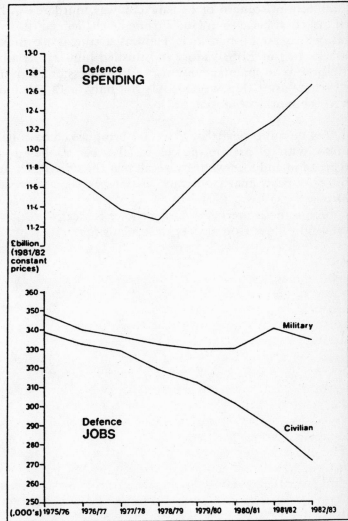

Source: TGWU Booklet, *A Better Future*

The twin devils of increasing injustice and arms expenditure face Christians with the greatest challenge to the reign of God in our age. They are the greatest countersign of the Kingdom, the chief negations of the gospel, that which more than anything else provokes God's judgement upon us.

Archbishop Romero of El Salvador was murdered in his own cathedral because in God's name he challenged those in authority to establish justice. He was a true peace maker amid the hell of El Salvador, and this led him into conflict with those who maintained injustice by repression, fear and the force of arms. His words apply not only to El Salvador, but to the world situation:

> Let us be quite clear that if we are being asked to collaborate with a pseudo peace, a false order, based on repression and fear we must recall that the only order and the only peace that God wants is one based on truth and justice.
>
> Before these alternatives, our choice is clear:
> We will follow God's order, not men's.[8]

[8]Bishop Colin Winter, *The Burden of Prophecy* S.C.M.

Rob Warner

From all appearances, Rob Warner could be just any other theological student, training for the Baptist ministry at Oxford. He, like many other students, is to be found 'locked in libraries', working towards finals.

But it was not so long ago that Rob oversaw the production of a ground-breaking book in Britain for Christians concerned about nuclear weapons. In fact, it was during work on *The Church and the Bomb* that Rob, then at Hodder and Stoughton, came more deeply to terms with the issues himself. Then an editor, now a writer, he has just completed a book entitled *Rediscovering the Spirit*, published by his former employers. He also serves as a consultant to *Renewal Magazine*.

In this chapter, Rob presents the argument that while the polarity between unilateralism and multilateralism is a false one, those who truly want peace must seek it 'on all sides and in all places'. Multilateralism of the past has achieved precious little; so a new understanding of the goal must be sought.

12: Multilateralism: What it Has Been and Could Be

Rob Warner

The nuclear threat is too great for the imagination to bear. We want to carry on with everyday living, with bringing up our children or pursuing our careers. And yet the balance of terror presses in on our happiness. Among the exquisite treasures of the Uddizi art gallery in Florence, among the age-old and untamed fells of the Lake District, and above all among people I love, one fleeting, poisonous thought has fractured my delight: all this could be smashed in an instant. Quite simply, in the words of W. L. Ury, director of Harvard University's Nuclear Negotiation Project, 'We live in a tinderbox.'

Rocks melt, lakes turn to ashes and great cities still smoulder while the dust clouds gather. Will this be the nuclear winter's last goodnight? The lasting memorial to humanity's lust after power could be a burnt out world.

Because the horror is so great, our minds seek refuge: politicians say the only alternative to current policies is suicidal madness. They tell us that nuclear weapons don't make war worse, they prevent it. Deterrence is set against naive pacifism, 'realistic' multilateralism against unilateral surrender. But is there a better alternative?

As Christians we accept such reassurance too quickly. I remember some years ago long discussions with an eloquent pacifist. She claimed the example of Christ left no room for weaponry. I argued that the witness of history confirmed the biblical doctrine of the Fall. As sure as eggs are eggs, nations will wage war.

In rejecting absolute pacifism as a reasonable policy for the state, I conveniently left nuclear weapons out of the picture. Much the same happened at a recent Tyndale conference on war. The quality of the papers and discussion was most envigorating. It was marvellous to see so much creative, biblical thought among evangelical academics. But nuclear weapons were generally lumped in with everything else. Much time was spent on the limitations of pacifism. This seemed reassuring. It implied that the only alternative to pacifism was the status quo.

It was left to John Stott to demonstrate that the use of nuclear weapons is incompatible with just war theory by pointing out that 1 – You cannot in a nuclear war ensure that the war is winnable; 2 – You cannot restrict your attack to military forces; 3 – You cannot ensure a strictly proportional response to aggression. In other words, there are two Christian approaches to war – just war and pacifism – but when it comes to nuclear war, both are in agreement. As an evangelical, if you want to obey the biblical mandate, either as a pacifist or as a just warrior, you need to be a nuclear pacifist.

Genuine multilateralism needs to be reclaimed by nuclear peacemakers. Too often multilateralism has been used as a cover by those who seek to propel the arms race. True multilateralism is the only means by which nations can together stop the race towards oblivion. In short, real multilateralism will be furthered when pacifists and just warriors stand arm in arm against nuclear weapons. We need multilateralists for peace.

Peace in our time

There has been no war in Europe for forty years. That is some achievement for this war-scarred continent. We are told this is thanks to nuclear weapons. The arsenal of the potential holocaust is portrayed as the instrument of lasting peace.

One cannot prove that weapons prevent war. They

certainly may have contributed to the tense peace of forty years. But the past is no guarantee against future war. We need a better basis than the arms race for long term peace. What's more, the theory of the deterrent would only need to be disproved once. But if the theory dies it will take millions of lives with it. The wages of the arms race threaten to be global death.

Many talk about 'the deterrent' as if it is a fixed quantity, costing a fixed amount and ensuring a stable peace. Quite simply, the deterrent as we know it, is by no means a fixed quantity. It's not that we possess just enough nuclear weaponry to prevent the other side using theirs. Nor are the stocks of armaments rising slowly. The arms race is in overdrive.

Take the case of France. In May 1985 President Mitterand launched The Inflexible. This submarine carries 96 nuclear warheads. Until then, the total number of warheads on all French subs was 'just' 48. These new missiles have a greater range, up from 3,000 to 4,500 km. That means reaching many more Russian targets from safe international waters. There will be 176 new warheads on French subs by the end of 1985, and 500 by 1992. Each warhead is equal to 150,000 tons of TNT. That means by 1992 the French alone could kill 60 million people – three times the Soviet losses against Hitler.

Such figures are horrific. But that's not all. Vice Admiral Coatanea, commander of the French Strategic Submarine Fleet has warned, 'It's all the missiles or none of them.' If France is attacked, full devastation will be unleashed. President Mitterand has said that French weapons will only be counted in at the Geneva arms talks when American and Russian missiles are at 'the lowest possible level'. Meanwhile, the French, like the British and like the superpowers, pour ever more money into the nuclear arms race.

In principle, the deterrent is not just to prevent the other side going nuclear. It is intended to prevent all manner of superpower conflict. Since it is believed that the Soviet block has superiority in conventional forces, NATO has a policy which states its willingness to use nuclear weapons first. Field Marshall Lord Carver, retired chief of British Defence staff, has described this policy as 'criminally irresponsible': it would surely trigger a Soviet response that would engulf the West.

Two more factors darken the equation. Like the French, the Russians have declared a policy of all or nothing. In other words, once a war goes nuclear, every missile is unleashed. If that's not bad enough, flight times for missiles are now very short. Decision time is down to minutes. The weapon systems and warning systems are increasingly computerized: to be effective at all, the whole nuclear stockpile is on a hairtrigger. This doesn't just mean that a faulty silicon chip could disgorge the world's end by mistake. A former Pentagon official has described a growing conviction not merely of all or nothing, but of strike first or you won't strike at all: 'In a real situation you don't compare going first to going second. You compare going first with not going at all . . . When you go, go. Do it. Finish the job. Launching under attack just means that you've missed the moment' (quoted in D. Ford *The Button* NY 1985).

As long as nuclear weapons are deemed to be acceptable and deemed to prevent all wars, the arms manufacturers are free to develop new weapon systems. These blur the boundary between nuclear and conventional war. NATO recently adopted a new policy – FOFA (Follow on Forces Attack). This harnesses emerging technologies for a deep counter-strike, 200 miles behind the enemy front line. The intention is to delay in war the 'need' to go nuclear first. Critics note that the aggressive policy contradicts NATO's official defensive intentions. What's more, this massive escalation of high tech weaponry, justified as delaying going nuclear, is *not* tied to the removal of a single NATO nuclear warhead from Western Europe. In short, it makes the arsenal of death bigger, more threatening and still more provocative.

The US army has a still more devastating policy. The Air-Land Battle Doctrine is committed to 'pre-emptive strikes at a potential enemy, ground attacks across borders, and the integrated use of conventional, chemical and nuclear arms' (*Newsweek* June 24 1985). The Russians are presumed to intend similar unspeakable vileness. Both are close to adding biological weapons to their arsenals.

Where boundaries are blurred, and ABC weapons (Atomic, Biological and Chemical) become part of our 'conventional' warfare, the risks of total escalation in the event of any war are massively increased. President Nixon put an American ban on new nerve gas weapons in 1969. Faced with evidence of Russian stockpiling, President Reagan has now set aside $124.5 million for producing a new nerve gas weapon. We are also on the brink of a chemical and biological arms race.

Superpower agreements

Surely multilateralism is against all this? In practice, the only thing multilateral has been immense stockpiling of arms. In preparation for negotiations, the superpowers build up stockpiles and work on new missiles to 'bargain from strength'. Such weapons are designed to be negotiated away as trade-offs. But the actual agreements have accepted all existing systems and approved even further expansion.

For example, the 1974 SALT I agreement could have banned MIRVs (many warheads on a single launch missile). The States had 832, Russia none. The Americans rejected a ban, and ceilings were agreed for five years of 1,808 new MIRV vehicles. Henry Kissinger later admitted he made no effort to set limits below what the States planned to build without any agreement. Overnight, maximum agreed levels became urgent production targets.

To gain Pentagon support for such treaties, internal concessions are made. The Defence Department is promised new armaments and the military research scientists are given more money to refine existing systems and develop still more nuclear weaponry. No doubt similar internal politics are found in the Kremlin.

The cost of 'bargaining chips' is staggering. Last April, the cost of keeping the MX on standby for Geneva, without producing the extra missiles wanted by President Reagan, was estimated at $1 billion. Mind you, over four years the Pentagon is spending at least $329 billion on defence, more than half on new weapons. Come economic boom or economic depression, inflation or deflation, high or low interest rates, every year is a growth year for the arms manufacturers, not least for those whose trade is nuclear terror.

Many of the scientists who made the first H-bomb regard the introduction of multiple warheads (MIRVs) as 'totally disastrous' and 'totally unnecessary' (*The Observer*, 19 May 1985). Dr Hans Bethe, Nobel prizewinner summed up that decision as 'driving out a demon by calling in the devil himself'. Forty years ago those scientists expected, at most, 200 US warheads if international negotiations *failed*. What we have now is 'absurd and obscene'.

One of these scientists recalled that in the mid-sixties the US Defence Department assessed how many warheads were needed. A group of scientific advisers said 200 was 'more than enough for every conceivable circumstance'. The Air Force wanted 2,000. The compromise was 1,000 – 'a nice round number that was not based on any rationale whatsoever'. Forty years after the two bombs of 1945, there are nearly 60,000 warheads. The megatonnage of death multiples every year.

Then there is the problem of the non-proliferation treaty. When it tested a 'peaceful nuclear device' in 1974, India joined the Club of Five (USA, USSR, China, UK, France). At least ten more countries are thought capable of building a nuclear bomb today. Some of these, probably including Israel and South Africa, have built bombs just short of completion. That way they avoid charges of illegal proliferation, but can finish warhead assembly within hours. Yet another twelve countries could have the bomb within the next five years.

Armaments often mean status. Leading two-thirds world countries now accuse the Club of Five of nuclear imperialism. If nuclear weapons prevent war, don't these countries have an equal right to possess them? Wouldn't this guarantee peace even more widely? The trouble is, no one trusts another country's nuclear arsenal.

The debate is beyond theoretical discussion. In 1985 India and Pakistan stare uncertainly across their borders, both uncomfortably certain that the other side possesses the Bomb.

In August 1985 the Indian minister for external affairs

warned, 'It is obvious that Pakistan's nuclear programme is not peaceful.' Two weeks later Pakistan's foreign minister counter-charged, 'The real threat comes from India . . . It has the admitted capacity and capability to produce nuclear weapons.'

Moral consequences

Multilateralism shows little evidence for slowing the arms race. It has by no means achieved reductions in arms stockpiles. But these are not the only results of living under the nuclear terror.

Arms mean money. Massive escalation means money for research and employment in a nation's arms industry. This means massive diversion of money away from social needs and the developing world. This is the first moral impact of the nuclear arms race.

Arms define an enemy. Nations have always depersonalized their enemies: the British have fought the Frogs and the Hun, the Commies and the Nazis. That is easier to cope with than killing people just like us. A policy of nuclear annihilation requires a depersonalization not just of the military and the politicians, but of all civilians: every pensioner and every schoolchild, every expectant mother and every baby at the breast.

Depersonalization goes even further. *The weapon of absolute destruction requires an absolute enemy for its target.* When President Reagan referred to Russia as the 'evil empire' he wasn't simply carried away by crusading rhetoric. He was giving witness to our universal fear of *their* weapons pointed at *us*. He was also giving witness to *our* 'moral' justification for pointing our weapons of mass destruction at *them*. For Russians, the nuclear tables are turned: President Reagan is the sinister mastermind ruling an empire just as threatening, and therefore just as evil. *Pravda* dismisses his strictures as 'another attack of an old disease – blind anticommunism'.

Total destruction annihilates morality. Mrs Thatcher has said civilized countries should have no dealings with those who pursue their political aims by force of arms and indiscriminate bloodshed. But our nuclear silos declare the threat of obliteration for all creatures great and small to be both justified and necessary. Our policies say that, if we were to be engulfed, the last and futile act of global destruction would actually make sense and actually be justified. Retaliation without proportion and without restraint, and even without hope of survival is the creed on which our political survival is staked.

Forty five years ago, an attack on civilians or even on a military ambulance was reprehensible. We defend our civilization with weapons more barbarous than the secular conventions of war recently permitted. A county schools inspector wrote to *The Times* in 1981 that 'surely in deploying such weapons, we erode the moral base' of the culture which we intend to defend.

Dreams and Fears

There is not merely a massive moral price to the arms race. The 'unthinkable' has for many become the 'inevitable'. That a nuclear doom awaits us is increasingly accepted. Fifteen years ago teenagers still looked to a future of increasing promise. Today, more and more are resigned and fatalistic. Why bother to make plans, why prepare for life beyond tomorrow, when a mushroom-shaped shroud looks set before the century's end to embrace us all?

This is a poisonous and wretched hopelessness. For the Christian, there is the ultimate reassurance that God is in control and that Christ will come again. But some of our contemporaries are learning to try to live with no future and no hope.

For many, total resignation is too much to bear. They escape instead into utopianism. The first utopia is the technological dream: We'll one day invent a weapon to end all wars. This hope is not only futile, but idolatrous. While we hope in the 'ultimate' weapon, research and development costs engulf whole societies. What's more, since World War II, Russia has always caught up with the West's advances.

The present utopian weapon is Star Wars. It may be able to shoot down nuclear warheads. Nobody knows yet. President Reagan has said it is strictly non-negotiable until fully developed and ready for implementation. This dream of peace through technology looks set to make the world even less safe: first, the Russians are likely to engage in massive nuclear build up on earth, to make the job of Star Wars more difficult and to bargain against it 'from strength'. Second, the Russians have warned it would be bound to cause a new arms race in space.

From the West's point of view, Star Wars is an attractive weapon. If it works, it will kill warheads, not people. But at the same time, the Americans are developing six new offensive nuclear systems. From the Russian point of view, the Pentagon clearly intends to neutralize the Soviet nuclear deterrent while *increasing* the American nuclear stockpile. In former Premier Andropov's words, this seems 'a bid to disarm the Soviet Union in the face of the US nuclear threat'. Seen from the East, Reagan's dream to be the President of Peace is aggressive and hypocritical.

The other utopian dream looks to human rather than technological perfection. Could we not reject such weapons outright and overnight? I believe Christians need to reject the use and ultimately the possession of these weapons, but I don't know any Christian *countries*! Neither superpower is going to accept a policy of total, unilateral nuclear disarmament. But there is room for unilateral initiatives within a multilateral policy geared to genuine arms reduction.

Britain and France have rejected having their nuclear stocks being counted in with the Americans in superpower talks. Once more this is surely most hypocritical and threatening seen from Moscow. Britain is in a position to resist escalation by rejecting the Trident programme before it is too late. We could also agree to count in our weapons, since we would hardly go nuclear alone.

Cruise missiles were introduced, not to counter a particular Soviet threat, nor as a bargaining chip for Geneva. The Europeans in NATO feared the States might stand aside from a European conflict. The Europeans therefore asked for Cruise as a decisive linkage, forcing the States to be implicated and involved. Any East-West conflict would therefore be intercontinental, not merely European. Here are new proportions to the nuclear nightmare. The arms race now escalates and we all grow more at risk, not merely to counter Soviet forces, but to tie the hands of our allies to the nuclear button.

I don't reject all unilateralism. But I cannot in all honesty see total unilateralism being a policy that would ever be enacted in the real world. When multilateral nuclear disarmament is affirmed as a goal of international negotiations, *then* there is clear room for unilateral measures to break the logjam of multilateral escalation.

Negotiation

Almost any kind of negotiation is geared not so much to fairness as to coming out on top. *Kramer versus Kramer* memorably showed how divorce proceedings can set ex-partners against each other, fighting for the best deal possible. Management and unions often want personal victories from their dealings. On both sides personal careers will be influenced by the kind of deal done. If someone does dare to suggest a strictly fair proposal, everyone tends to distrust it or put it down to a weak bargaining position.

This priority of self assumes its darkest colours when making deals over nuclear death. We have seen how bargaining counters tend not to be given up. We negotiate from strength, but then retain that surplus strength, and even legalize further escalation. Recently on Capitol Hill the difficult process of learning to cooperate even *within* a country was described: The White House was said to be finally 'learning that neither of us is going to get anything done without some degree of cooperation'. How much more difficult to make a deal with those seen as holding the ultimate threat, set square against us as our ultimate enemy.

True multilateralism demands the priority of peace. True multilateralism needs urgently to press for a freeze on missile development and a ban on nuclear testing. True multilateralism needs to pursue fast and hard a massive, balanced reduction in nuclear stockpiles, and an urgent return to single warhead missiles.

Nuclear arms cannot be disinvented. If they were all taken apart, easy re-assembly would still be possible. But at the very least we should argue for a measure of sanity. At the very least we should call for urgent multilateral reduction of nuclear arms to a level deemed the minimum for mutual deterrence. Such a deterrent would serve one single purpose: not to claim the impossible and prevent all wars, but simply to prevent the use of nuclear weapons themselves.

Will the superpowers ever agree to multilateral peace-making? Many doubt it. The military/arms manufacturers complex has a will of its own. It's hard to say 'no' to the latest weapons' technology. But the power to say 'no' lies with the people. We need to remember World War I. Europe slipped into a war nobody wanted when sanity was forgotten in a frenetic arms race. They called it 'The war to end all wars'. If we fail to learn the lessons of history, we may be condemned to repeat its tragic bloodshed on a global and terminal scale. For the carnage of the Somme and Ypres, read the carnage of Moscow and Kiev, New York, Paris and London.

Conclusions

Nuclear war is so appalling our minds switch off. Only as we read of the experience of Hiroshima and Nagasaki, only as we turn cold statistics into the agony of the firestorm or the utter degradation of radiation poisoning, only as we feel the horror of nuclear death, not as military theory but as a living, demonic threat, only then can we begin to assess multilateralism. Only then can we stop shrugging our shoulders. Only then can we stop leaving the problem to others.

Evangelicals have tended to be stronger on personal morality than wider issues of justice and peace. Those who stand against abortion on demand recognize the massacre of countless babies to be a terrible affront to their human value and to the love of our Creator God. We need also to recognize the terrible affront stored in the silos and missiles of the superpowers.

The world is still in the hands of the Creator and Sovereign God. Ultimate peace between God and sinful people is secure in the death and resurrection of Christ. As those who have received the gift of peace with God, we need to proclaim that peace. We need also to pray for peace and work for peace against the demonic destructiveness of the Bomb.

Pacifist or just warrior? It is a false divide. As Christians we stand united in moral rejection of the use of the Bomb. Unilateralist or multilateralist? It is another false divide. We stand together against the arms race. We stand together, at the very least, for massive reduction of the nuclear stockpiles.

We urgently need to reclaim multilateralism from those who keep negotiating *increases* in the arms race. The only multilateralism worth the name calls upon the people of the world to rise up against the nuclear obscenity. We either work hard and pray hard for peace, or we wash our hands of God's created world and leave it to the experts to negotiate us out of existence. Those 'experts' will keep accelerating the arms race until by accident or by 'military wisdom' or by madness, the nuclear button is finally pushed.

Pilate washed his hands but could not evade responsibility. We are without excuse, before God and before each other if we ignore an issue of such immensity. Those called to true peace need to live and work as true peacemakers.

I saw on TV recently an American pastor praying God's blessing on newly made cruise missiles as instruments of godly peace. I wanted to weep. All evangelicals are called to be peacemakers. I believe all evangelicals need to link arms of prayer and arms of defiance against the blasphemy of the Bomb.

Dana Mills-Powell

An American by birth though not a believer in its dream, Dana Mills-Powell is a relative newcomer to Britain. She came here in 1982 from Sojourners Fellowship in Washington, DC where she co-founded the Peace Ministry and assisted in the publication of four books or study guides on nuclear weapons. She expects to receive her M.A. in peace studies from the University of Bradford in the spring of 1986.

Dana's entry into issues of nuclear weapons and peace came through her association with Sojourners magazine and through meeting a man named Bob Aldridge. Dana describes that meeting in her chapter and also some of the issues which meeting him raised for her. She firmly believes that while some Christians would attempt to avoid the issues around nuclear weapons, it is, for us in this time, an issue of faith which tests what we say about Jesus as Lord.

13: Calling Bluffs in a Nuclear Age

Dana Mills-Powell

'OK kids, down under the desks.'

I knew it was just for practice, but all the same, I was afraid. For one very long minute, the classroom was completely silent, except for the ticking of the large clock. Crouched under my desk, all I could look at were the little dots in the floor tiles, and wait for my teacher's beckoning us back into normality. Fire drills were never like this, I remember thinking, since I knew a fire couldn't keep me away from my family and my dog. Life would go on after a fire.

I grew up, like millions of others in my generation, in a nuclear age. We were forced to face the horrors of nuclear war before we even faced the meaning of death at all. My memories of the exercise in the classroom were during the weeks around the 1962 Cuban missile crisis. Though I didn't understand the political confrontation going on, I did understand that danger was all around us and that President Kennedy was doing what he could to keep us all safe. That was all that mattered to a seven year old American kid.

In the years that followed, drills and exercises became part and parcel of going to school in America. Being on one's best behaviour during these exercises was what we could do to love our country, to show we were proud to be Americans. The reality of the dangers which faced us was never more poignant when all the children in my school walked home in groups, escorted by teachers, to prepare for the possibility of loss of transport during war. I'm now sure that what was really being prepared were our attitudes – even in nuclear war we would be able to get home, despite not having our school buses!

Atomic and nuclear weapons sank deeply into the background of life during the late 60s and 70s. Except for an occasional fall-out shelter sign, I was not reminded of the dangers of nuclear war until I was in college. It was there that I met a man named Bob Aldridge.

It was a soft, spring evening in 1977 when Bob drove into the car park at Westmont College in Santa Barbara, California with his wife Janet and at least three of their ten children. As I walked up to meet their car, a passerby noticed a sticker, 'Live Without Trident' on their car window and asked me, 'What's so bad about Trident chewing gum?' Such was the level of awareness around the US Navy's newest submarine system which Bob had helped design during his employment at Lockheed Space and Missile Company.

During that first evening meal together, I found Bob and Janet to be refreshingly simple people, yet full of integrity. Little did I know back then that Bob's intimate knowledge of the Trident system and US defense policies would propel me into an active involvement in opposing the very things I had grown up blindly accepting. And little did he probably know that his knowledge, which led to his resignation from Lockheed four years earlier, would also eventually put him at the forefront of the movement against nuclear weapons.

Over the next two days, I escorted Bob to various classes and meetings to speak about his observations and concerns related to his development in the aerospace industry. While I was horrified at what Bob spoke about, I was also deeply moved by his act of conscience in leaving a lucrative engineering job after 20 years of employment, with ten children in his and Janet's care. He shared how he could simply not see the compatibility of the work he was doing with his Christian faith. What he had been doing, he described in full detail, as he has in his book, *First Strike*:

'Design studies on the first Polaris missile were just getting underway when I hired-on on at Lockheed. As we advanced through three generations of Polaris and into the Poseidon submarine-launched weapons, I became a veteran engineer on sea-based missiles and leader of an advanced design group. At that time I valued my work, but how it was evaluated troubled me: the Poseidon weapons system was given an 'effectiveness rating' of 80 million fatalities. Still, I looked upon America as the hope of the world, and I put my work in service to that ideal.'[1]

Bob was elevated in his work in the early 1970s to develop multiple warheads on single weapons as a means of getting round the SALT I treaty limits on nuclear weapons. Although Bob saw the hypocrisy of such a plan, he now believes that 'my moral qualms were not strong enough to override my attachment to the weekly paycheck'.[2] Next it was to the development of MARVs, or manoeuvring re-entry vehicles, which could evade enemy interceptors during flight. It was during work on the MARVs that he began to see the direction of US policies more clearly:

'To update my knowledge on manoeuvring technology I reviewed numerous secret documents. I soon discovered that Pentagon strategists have a keen interest in more accurate weapons . . . the precision they desired could only be useful for destroying hardened targets such as missile emplacements or command posts. This was a departure from our stated deterrent policy of only firing when fired upon . . . I was unhampered in my perception that going after the Soviet's land-based missiles meant shooting first because it made no sense to retaliate against empty silos. I was also outraged that this move toward first strike was kept secret from the public.'[3]

This move towards 'first strike' of which Aldridge writes is a dangerous development in weapons technology. Although the terminology has become common, the eventu-

[1]Robert C. Aldridge, *First Strike*, Boston, MA, South End Press, p. 14.
[2]Ibid., p. 15.
[3]Ibid.

ality in a nuclear age is extremely threatening. Aldridge defines it as 'a capability to inflict a *disarming* or *unanswerable* attack against a rival nation'. While some similarities exist with traditional military strategy, what makes a nuclear first strike distinct is the finality of it; it is impossible for the attacked to retaliate.

First strike is not to be confused with 'first use' which is the description of whatever country initiates nuclear war, often associated with a 'limited use' of nuclear weapons to stop a massive attack with conventional armaments. Nor is it to be confused with 'counterforce' which is to aim attack missiles at military targets; '*counter*ing the enemy *forces*'. While all first strike weapons are counterforce weapons (aimed at military targets), not all counterforce are first strike. This is because there are degrees of counterforce. For example, the ability to destroy bomber bases would require counterforce weapons or counterforce targeting. But destroying a bomber base does not constitute a disarming strike because silo-based and submarine based missiles would be certain to retaliate. Therefore, a disarming first strike capability can be described as the ultimate in counterforce.[4]

In spite of the fact that these definitions read to many of us as mere theorising, to Bob Aldridge they were shattering new realizations about his field of work which demanded a response. The fact that the United States was moving intentionally toward obtaining this first strike capability meant he had to face not only an issue of life and death, but one of his Christian faith.

The Question To Be Asked

In my nine years of working with these issues, I have spoken to many people about what we face as citizens of a nuclearized nation, but primarily as followers of Jesus. Many questions and comments are put to me about my stance against nuclear weapons, but there is one which surfaces most often:

But nuclear weapons act as a deterrent to war; they prevent war from occurring at all.

[4]Ibid., p. 25.

While most people in Britain believe that current military strategy is based on deterrence, this is not the policy which undergirds NATO strategy. Deterrence took on the name 'mutually assured destruction' (MAD) in the 1970s, which stated US intentions to inflict massive destruction on Russian cities in the event of a nuclear attack. MAD was a policy of retaliation which, in the minds of Pentagon strategists, would keep the Russians from ever initiating a nuclear war.

But deterrence has been put to rest by a more aggressive posture towards superpower military bluffs. Basic to American policy and, according to defense analysts, Soviet as well, is the concept of counterforce. The difference between the two approaches is what the weapons are aimed at: where MAD targeted cities, counterforce targets military sites. And that makes all the difference. For as Aldridge stated, what use is it to destroy empty missile silos? Counterforce is, by definition, a policy which requires shooting *first*.

So once such a policy becomes operational in terms of military strategy, the overriding goal is to achieve a winning formula – to have enough of a first strike capability to achieve 'victory'. But, you may say, there is no evidence that this is what is behind US or NATO policy. One would wish it were so.

The Hard Evidence

As early as 1960, the Pentagon had begun to draw up its plans for a total, complete, pre-emptive strike capability on the Soviet Union. Called the Single Integrated Operational Plan (SIOP), it assigns every nuclear weapon to a specific target in the USSR. Among them are:

> Soviet strategic retaliatory forces such as missile silos, bomber bases and submarine tenders.
>
> Soviet air defences away from cities which would cover US bomber routes.
>
> Soviet command and control centres and systems.[5]

[5]Ibid. p. 27–8. Aldridge is quoting from Ball, Desmond, *Deja Vu: The Return to Counterforce in the Nixon Administration*, (California Seminar on Arms Control and Foreign Policy, December 1974), pp. 10–13.

While this shift in targeting is not often admitted by U.S. or NATO officials, when it is the implications are often clouded. In 1962 when SIOP was adopted, then Defence Secretary McNamara made the first official reference to a counterforce capability: 'A major mission of the strategic retaliatory forces is to deter war by their capability to destroy the enemy's warmaking capabilities.'[6] While he admits the shift in targeting, he attempts to define the policy as 'retaliatory.' An unnamed McNamara aide was more to the point: 'There could be no such thing as a primary retaliation against military targets after an enemy attack. If you're going to shoot at missiles, you're talking about first strike.'[7]

What other evidence of counterforce do we see at work? Namely, in the weapons systems of the superpowers. In the U.S., it was in 1967 when McNamara changed the emphasis on weapons procurement from quantity to quality that the shift in policy began to have an effect. This enabled the entire military-industrial complex to develop better, rather than bigger, missiles – with the capability of destroying hardened Soviet targets. This required almost pinpoint accuracy, whereby destroying cities in a retaliatory strike required only a 'big bang.' That qualitative shift was quickly mirrored in Moscow, thus making the numbers game of the NATO/Warsaw pact balance obsolete. The cutting edge of the new arms race is the smart, rather than the big, bomb.

This effort towards better bombs required new weapons systems for every leg of the US strategic triad – land, sea, and air. The new 'generation' of weapons resulted in plans for the M-X (land-based, but mobile rather than stationary), Trident (submarine system; able to destroy 435 different hardened targets; at least four are currently deployed in the Pacific Northwest of the U.S.), and cruise missiles (undetectable by enemy radar and extremely accurate). Each weapons system takes the arms race into new and dangerous territory.

Most defence analysts agree that the Soviets are most threatening in terms of their cumulative lethal capability –

[6]Ibid., p. 28, as quoted from Department of Defense Appropriations for 1963, hearings before the House Appropriations Committee, (January 1962), Part 2, pp. 249–250.
[7]Ibid, as quoted in *Deja Vu*, p. 15.

their explosive power far exceeds that of NATO forces. But that does not compare with the sophistication of NATO's technological capability. Despite that disadvantage, one must assume that the Soviets are also working towards a counterforce capability in developing weapons systems like the SS-18 and 20 – extremely dangerous ICBMs (intercontinental ballistic missiles).

Other evidence of the US commitment to counterforce became clear in 1980. While counterforce was very much an accepted doctrine among military planners and design engineers, still there was no official statement which reflected this commitment. It was President Carter who signed the Presidential Directive-59 and then Defence Secretary Harold Brown who defended it: 'PD-59 is not a new strategic doctrine; it is not a radical departure from U.S. strategic policy over the past decade or so. It is, in fact a refinement, a codification of previous statements of our strategic policy.'[8] Emphasising a 'countervailing strategy', PD-59 states the need for 'flexibility' in targeting.

Capability or Intention?

But still a fundamental question remains: even if NATO and the U.S. have the first strike *capability*, that doesn't mean that they will ever *use* it. This is a difficult leg to stand on, most simply because every weapon that has ever been invented has been used – one cannot be optimistic if one takes history – or the Bible – seriously. In addition, as the Soviet Union attempts to match U.S. development for a greater strategic counterforce capability, the situation becomes more volatile – and the pressure towards a first strike grows. In fact, there is a commitment growing on both sides to adopt a policy of 'launch on warning' so that the minute an attack is detected, weapons are fired. This is the only way that missiles aren't 'sitting ducks' for the supposed on-coming attack.

Propelled by massive commitments to their military industrial complex, each superpower continues to fuel this

[8]Ibid., p. 35, as taken from remarks by Harold Brown at Naval War College on August 20, 1980.

arms race in the name of national security. But increasingly
they know that their people are growing weary and afraid.
Whereby the rationale in previous decades for new developments in the arms race was the threat of the other side,
increasingly we are beginning to see that the new rationale
is for 'peace'. The existence of nuclear weapons is taken for
granted in practice, thereby the effort is towards making us
'safer' in their shadow. Nothing apart from a slow, but
thorough, process of dismantling these weapons will make
the world safer – taking the war to space only provides the
superpowers with new vistas for weapons development.

The Pulse of Life

Six months ago I was privileged to participate with God
and with my husband in the miracle of giving birth. No
other experience has taught me more about the preciousness
of life. Seven years of working for peace – speaking, writing,
organizing, going to jail – all of it came to a miraculous
climax in the months around Bridget's birth. I remember
one day in early summer in 1985 when we were in prayer
with others from the Evangelical Peacemakers network.
Much of our prayer had been reflecting the pain of the world,
the groaning of creation. Suddenly, inside me, there was a
hop, skip, and a jump! Life and hope would not be put
asunder! I was awed by the message this little, unborn child
offered to us, and tried desperately to communicate it to my
brothers and sisters through tears of joy.

We are all invited to join in with this pulse of life, but,
like Bob Aldridge, we all have choices to make. One is
whether we will 'leave it to the experts'. To do so would
not be simply choosing to remain silent – for silence in the
face of such a crisis is actually giving our consent. Nor is
mere opposition a choice for responsible Christians. Jesus
was and is the Word becoming flesh – so must our words
take on our flesh. And this will require *acts* of non-cooper-
ation. When Caesar asks of us something which we cannot
give – our industrial and creative capacities, our countrysides
now laden with barbed wire, our children's future, all for

an illusion of security — we must do what we must do, and live faithfully with the consequences.

We are as Christians people who are propelled by hope. We have the privilege of setting our sights on a vision of life over death, even as seen in the life of one small baby. The more we live into that vision, the more we will see it begin to take shape around us.

Roger Forster

It was in 1974 when a small group of Christians began to evangelize in South East London, and Ichthus Fellowship was born. Today the church is one of the most well known of the house churches, although it is not part of either of the two main fellowship 'circles' in this country. Roger Forster ('Mr, please, not Rev') is their leader and pastor – a man well respected throughout the evangelical community. Someone once described him as 'a bridge between the established denominations and the house churches'. Another[1] described him as having 'one of the finest minds in the Evangelical constituency that I have ever encountered'.

In this chapter, Roger offers some truths learned from the life of his fellowship as they have struggled with issues of war and peace. He emphasises the importance of opinions being subject to the bonds of Christ that knit the church together. In so doing, he presents some lively questions not only for the church, but also for all who would call themselves peacemakers.

[1] Andrew Walker, *Restoring the Kingdom*: The Radical Christianity of the House Church Movement, Hodders, London, 1985.

14: The Church that Makes for Peace

Roger Forster

I am one who holds a tremendous respect for those in the military. This is partly from my own positive experiences in the Royal Air Force, back in the 1950s. We experienced a mini-revival, selling 160 large Bibles in six weeks to the many converts from amongst the RAF personnel. I even managed to pray with the commanding officer one day after requesting to put a Gospel message through the p.a. system throughout the whole of the camp. He said to me, 'You know Forster, we don't want to give the men too much religion do we?' I replied, 'If we want to know whether it is too much religion or not sir, we ought to pray about it.' He seemed a little taken aback and said, 'Well, you pray.' I did not know whether he meant immediately on the spot or whether he meant I was to go away and pray. Anyway, I took the bull by the horns and removing my military beret, prayed aloud, asking the Lord to let us know whether the p.a. broadcast would be too much religion for the men. Then I put my beret on, saluted and marched out. I soon had my reply, not only from God but from the commanding officer. We were able to broadcast every night for five minutes. How could he refuse after such an exercise?!

While I hold all military personnel in high regard, I have a particular admiration for the faith of Christian servicemen. While I recognize that the problems of their calling have increased with the growing investment in nuclear weapons, my respect for such individuals has not diminished. On the other hand, my understanding of Jesus' mind regarding peace and violence has developed through the years and is in some degree in conflict with the position that someone in the military would probably take. However, I will not allow this conflict to destroy the fundamental peace which our Lord won for us at the price of His blood.

> . . . and through Him to reconcile to Himself all things, whether things on earth or things in heaven, by making peace through His blood, shed on the cross. Once you were alienated from God and were enemies in your minds because of your evil behaviour. But now He has reconciled you by Christ's physical body through death to present you holy in His sight, without blemish and free from accusation – if you continue in your faith, not moved from the hope held out in the Gospel. This is the Gospel that you heard and that has been proclaimed to every creature under heaven, and of which I, Paul, have become a servant. (Col 1:20–23)

God is a god of reconciliation and this means that I must also be reconciled to those whose ideas are alien, or even hostile, to mine. My commitment must be to the whole of that creation which the Lord Jesus has reconciled to Himself (Col 1:21–23). We are all in the one body, called to be a prophetic people of peace.

Prophetic People of Peace

In the Sermon on the Mount (Matt 5–7), Jesus gives His first definition of the church, the prophetic people of God. Addressing the crowd, he describes His people as a blessed people, a happy people. One of His descriptions is 'happy are the peacemakers for they shall be called the sons[2] of God'. Undoubtedly they received this name because they expressed, as offspring of God, His peaceful, reconciling character. Then Jesus goes on to address personally those

---

[2]Author prefers 'sons' to 'children' as translated in some texts.

who through their relationship with Him, will find themselves persecuted. He says they are prophets like those of the Old Testament who were also persecuted. The church committed to Jesus and bearing His name is to be a prophetic people, an instrument for God speaking into the world. As we fulfil this calling we act like salt and light. We are like a city set on a hill that cannot be hidden. Our lives and words bring glory to the Father.

In order to fulfil this prophetic ministry to which Christ has called us, we need to do more than hurl verbal broadsides at the secular governments or societies in which we live. Like the Old Testament prophets, four-fifths of our prophetic ministry will be to God's community and only one-fifth to the nations or those not regarded as God's people. Even that one-fifth will not be effective unless it arises from a community which is obviously living out the other four-fifths of the prophetic word.

Our verbal protests against a disregard for life must be heard and seen as coming from a body of people who are demonstrating that it is possible to live in peace. Self-righteous superiority, intellectually proud paternalism, or even hypocritical Pharisaism, could be charges brought against even sincere Christian protest which is not coming from a community of reconciliation, peace and love. It is clear that our desire for world peace as portrayed in Zechariah 9:9–11 or Isaiah 2:1–5, will not be fulfilled by waiting passively for Christ's return, but by our living now the values and character of His Kingdom. By this we show that we want a world where the war machine is destroyed and peace exists among the nations.

As twentieth century Christians, however, we have a long way to go. Where are the communities of peace-loving, peace-living, peace-speaking people, in which the reality of the reconciliation Jesus has won for us is truly expressed, namely that in Christ 'there is neither Jew nor Greek, slave nor free, male or female, for you are all one in Christ Jesus' (Gal 3:28)? Only a body of believers where discrimination has disappeared – where race, colour, sex, education, economic standing, culture and religious advantages have given way – has the right and power to be God's prophetic voice to the world. Among believers, Christ must *be* all and *in* all. Sometimes the prophecy will be a tearful one, as Jesus' was in Luke 19:41–44.

'As He approached Jerusalem and saw the city, He wept over it and said "If you, even you, had only known this day what would bring you peace – but now it is hidden from your eyes. The days will come upon you when your enemies will build an embankment against you and encircle you and hem you in on every side. They will dash you to the ground, you and the children within your walls. They will not leave one stone on another, because you did not recognize the time of God's coming to you." '

When the source of peace is denied and the motivation of some protagonists has to be questioned, the discernment of spirits becomes a necessary gift confined not only to spiritual meetings, but to the wider sphere of our contact with the world. In order to guard the flock from alien forces and deception, it requires understanding and guidance from the Holy Spirit, so that those destructive spirits do not destroy God's community of peace. In practical terms therefore, we encourage the widest fellowship between Christians who stand on peace platforms and those who do not, in order that peace might be the basic rule of our relationships in Christ and not hostility.

Seek Ye First

Nonetheless, we urge that the higher way is to seek the interests of the Kingdom of God, which will not be advanced by the use of the sword. The interests of God's Kingdom were declared by Jesus when He preached from Isaiah 61:2. This was on the occasion of His visit to His home town and its local synagogue.

The Spirit of the Lord is upon Me, because He anointed Me to preach the Gospel to the poor. He has sent Me to proclaim release to the captives, and recovery of sight to the blind, to set free those who are down-trodden, to proclaim the favourable year of the Lord. (Luke 4:18–19.

He told stories of God's activity and blessing amongst non-Israelites. God seemed magnificently unconcerned with religious privileges and national boundaries, dispersing His blessings irrespectively. Widows, lepers, and those of foreign nations were privileged recipients of His bounty, much to the disgust of Jesus' hearers (Lk 4:20–27), who sought to execute Him by throwing Him over the nearby cliff. This destructive intention was thwarted by supernatural protection. God reigned; His Kingdom was at hand (Lk 4:28–30). At least six factors emerge in this incident which direct us, as Jesus' followers, in the pursuit which He has placed before us; 'Seek first the Kingdom' (Mt 6:33).

● The *anointing* of the Holy Spirit was essential for Jesus if He was to proclaim and express the Kingdom of God. Our involvement with this same Holy Spirit, the Dove of God, is also essential if the Kingdom of God is to appear (cf: Rom 14:17 'The Kingdom of God is . . . peace in the Holy Spirit'). So the first target of our Fellowship is to see as many people as possible born again into, then baptized and filled, with the Holy Spirit. This locates the fountain of peace within the church and so begins to change the spiritual atmosphere of the immediate area, borough, city, nation and, so we anticipate, the world.

Our church has discovered that the very atmosphere which non-Christians breathe can be changed by the presence and activity of Spirit-filled worshippers. The church becomes the source of a new peaceful spirit for the people to breathe and imbibe instead of breathing the aggressive and violent spirit of the age. We have found this has taken place not only amongst a few neighbours in ordinary situations but also when the community has been teetering on the verge of rioting in our inner-city areas. Worshipping while marching together in the open air, and preaching in the context of celebration has defused fear and threats of violence and brought smiles back to people's faces.

The encouragement which comes from the Wind of God,

and the air of Heaven makes it possible for people to learn the way of peace. Attitudes change and also the climate of opinion concerning violence, even nuclear destruction. On the other hand, the effects of aggressive and violent protest will only stir up anger and unrest, unmasking the source of even nuclear obliteration.

• *Prisoners are released* when God's Kingdom is on the move. There is liberty for the captive; those who were blinded in dark dungeons are brought out into the light (Is 61:1–2). To cast out evil spirits in people and society; to bind authorities in the name of Jesus, to release slaves of ignorance into the light of understanding God's mind are all functions of a Kingdom people. By such aggressive activity the church opposes the armies of destructive spirits and challenges the spiritual principalities of nuclear warfare with God's reigning over them in Jesus' name. If we add to all this an actual prison ministry supported by the church community, then the nation may soon be challenged by released ex-convicts demanding a hearing for peace.

• God's Kingdom is *good news to the poor*. Of course this means that the church purse ensures no one is in need (Acts 2:45, 4:35); but more than this, the poor, those devoid of power to implement their will or decisions, are now able to do so by the power of the Holy Spirit and prayer. Jesus says:

'Have faith in God. Truly I say to you, whoever says to this mountain. "Be taken up and cast into the sea" and does not doubt in his heart, but believes that what he says is going to happen, it shall be granted him. Therefore I say to you, all things for which you pray and ask, believe that you have received them, and they shall be granted you.' (Mk 11:22–24)

Also, in John 14:13 the possibilities opened up by prayer in Jesus' name seem limitless. Advancing by success on smaller fronts, as we have been discovering, the church can be encouraged to take on the nuclear issue.

• A major demonstration of God's reign is in the *healing* of bodies and broken hearts. (Is 61:1–2, Lk 9:1–4, 10:9). Peace in the body and peace of heart and mind are fundamental denials of physical destruction and fear. The healing ministry of the Church reveals that God is on the side of life, and He commands 'fear not' more times than anything else. To see God working actively in the direction of healing challenges the world view of the 'destroyers of the earth'. Hopefully it stimulates a 'fear of the Lord' in the latter instead of their fear in humanity, and might even bring them into wisdom (Proverbs 9:10).

● The whole Kingdom era is called the *'acceptable year' of the Lord'* (AV). This was understood in terms of the Old Testament Jubilee year in which the people of God gave each other freedom, peace, and rest, accepting each other as God had accepted them. Jesus now offers such a jubilee across the divisions of national self-interest. It was for this reason that His fellow Israelites wished to destroy Jesus, throwing Him over the cliff. Serious Kingdom seekers will today work to express God's mind of a supra-national people, devoid of that sort of national self-interest which is at the expense of others. They will also work to ensure that a people in which there is neither 'Jew nor Greek, Parthian or Scythian' as Paul puts it, is demonstrable to all nations of the earth. By joining hands across the world and giving each other the jubilee acceptance of peace and 'shalom', we will be able to check and challenge world opinion as to the relevance of the bomb. It will seem useless for national advantage and irrelevant by the universal presence of another kind of humanity.

It has often been said that the success of Wilberforce in abolishing slavery was due to his parliamentary acumen and ability. Some of us think otherwise. Things only began to change when he, with God's people, set about informing the minds of the ordinary populace. When the public was informed and therefore changed, so parliamentarians had to change. Could not a world force of supra-national, peace-loving and peace-living, world-communicating sons and daughters of God change world opinion? Even if some powerful or evil persons remain unconvinced these can still be over-ruled by God's reign.

● Just as Jesus overruled and *walked through the crowd's antagonism*, so we as a Fellowship engage in aggressive spiritual warfare. Yet we believe that vengeance belongs to the Lord and not to us. We do anticipate God's intervention to fight for us and believe that the end times will see more of what we call 'holy war' that is, supernatural warfare, in the defence and advancement of God's interests on the earth.

Barriers to Peace

It is important, therefore, that we deal with those things that hinder our corporate witness to the peace and reconciliation that Jesus brings. In Mark 9:50, Jesus says to His disciples, 'Have salt in yourselves and be at peace with one another.' This statement follows two incidents where the disciples were plainly not expressing God's peace in their behaviour and activities. Firstly, they were arguing among themselves as to which of them was the greatest. Secondly, they recounted to Jesus how they had forbidden someone to cast out demons in His name because the man did not belong to their little band. Thirdly, the parallel passage in Luke 9 adds an incident in which James and John wanted to call down fire from Heaven to punish a Samaritan village which had not received Jesus. These three incidents show us graphically the causes of warfare on a private, public and national scale.

Firstly, there is misdirected *ambition*. The drive to succeed in the world, to make our mark, is not in itself rebuked by Jesus but only when it is used to lord it over our fellows in order to become 'top dog'. Instead, Jesus exhorts us to channel our ambitious energy into serving one another and the world. Our fellowship life in Christ's Church should be teaching and helping us to destroy our private dreams for pre-eminence and competition. Freed from these we will approach the world, and its opposing opinions, securely. We will come with no desire to make a name for ourselves, to put down our protagonists and humiliate them, nor indeed to outshine our own colleagues. If, in the therapeutic community of Jesus, we practice the menial and unnoticed service; if we promote our brothers and sisters in the family by commendatory words and prayer; if our prayers are those which ask that God's grace might bless and shine out from our Christian colleagues in more measure than from ourselves, then we will be fit to speak out against the bomb and commend the 'way of peace'. We will be showing that this way is possible, and that we have found it.

Children are especially important in this therapy. Jesus shows us this by holding one in the midst of the disciples (Mk 9:36). While we are trying to be big and have first place we cannot see children; we overlook them. To receive one, on the other hand, is to receive Jesus and His Father. What kind of greatness towards which we may aspire can out-class that?

Our fellowship's leadership was involved in a dispute between two official parties over a backward child. The youngster was being used to create a confrontation. One of our members who was in the front line of the controversy came to us for prayer. He reported to us that one party had totally dismissed the boy's value. I asked, 'Where does God stand in this issue?' After a few moments' reflection he said, 'God thinks a lot of children doesn't He?' I replied, with verses such as these in Mark 9, 'His Kingdom is made up of them.' So we both knew how to pray. I also advised him to use the name of Jesus publicly when he put his view forward saying that this is God's view of children. Throughout the dispute which transpired the next day we prayed every hour, receiving reports on how to direct our praying. We have no doubt that at the end of the day, despite threats and calls for action, the intervention of God on behalf of a little backward boy saved him from grave misfortune.

The nuclear issue is not different, even if it is on a larger scale. What God thinks about innocent children (much more than adults who have had the major portion of their time, yet are threatening to destroy, maim or irradiate millions of the next generation) is not too difficult to ascertain. He will destroy those who destroy the earth (Rev 11:18). We know whose side God is on and we know too our true greatness when we receive children and seek to serve them with a hope for the future. Of course we can hardly serve the current generation of children, or be understood to be receiving them in Jesus' name, if we try to protect them from the bomb while exposing them to other forms of destruction like abortion. The reverse is equally true. The Lord gives us children to receive and serve that we may be truly great.

Secondly, He warns against the *pride* and spiritual superiority that causes us to separate from others who work in the name of Jesus, and confine religious privileges and authority to a select few. Pride about our own privileged position and understanding will expose us to Satan, our enemy, and lead us to defeat. Furthermore, the same pride will assert itself when we confront the non-christian world and its leaders with the issues of the bomb. Too often the moral superiority of our case breathes through us in a self-righteous, pharisaical patronage. In comparison, our antagonists are often made to appear almost saints, far more attractive in the eyes of the average person – and maybe also in the eyes of God! Even worse, perhaps, is when we denigrate or even resist the genuine work of another believer whom really we should be helping.

However, there is more in this incident of Mark 9:38–40 and the instruction given by our Lord, than just an attack on denominational superiority and pride. The man in question was actually doing miracles in Jesus' name. In fact if he had not been doing miracles the apostles would possibly have welcomed him with open arms and joined forces with him. At least it seems to be the case in many quarters of the Christian camp today. Possibly in some way John felt threatened by the stranger's ministry of power, even though he had performed a few miracles himself in his time. How much more those with less 'spectacular' ministries today feel threatened when a powerful ministry appears. Thousands of reasons or excuses are found for rejecting such a ministry or even vilifying it as being of the devil. But Jesus said, 'No one who does a miracle in my name can in the next moment say anything bad about me.'

In our work in London, Matthew 11:20–24 has become an important text for us.

'Then Jesus began to denounce the cities in which most of His miracles had been performed, because they did not repent. 'Woe to you, Korazin! Woe to you, Bethsaida! If the miracles that were performed in you had been performed in Tyre and Sidon, they would have repented long ago in sack-cloth and ashes. But I tell you, it will be more bearable for Tyre and Sidon on the day of judgment than for you. And you, Capernaum, will you be lifted up to the skies? No, you will go down to the depths. If the miracles that were performed in you had been performed in Sodom, it would have remained to this day. But I tell you that it will be more bearable for Sodom on the day of judgment than for you.'

This challenges us to mighty works if we are going to re-evangelize London. If Sodom would have repented, if the people had seen Jesus' miraculous ministry, then presumably London could have a good chance too if we were moving in even a small part of the same power. Jesus does seem to encourage such an expectation (Jn 14:12).

We must stand in awe of Jesus' words concerning those working in His name, but who are not 'of us'. We will also recognize the need for some brothers and sisters to move in signs and wonders. It is when these conditions pertain, that we are in a position to challenge, with the miraculous, people and world leaders involved with the nuclear war machine. There is no need to assume that their hearts are harder than Sodom (cf: Genesis 19). Mighty works should awe them to repentance.

It is unlikely that we can bring the fear of the Lord to those responsible for the bomb unless we also fear Jesus' words concerning love and unity. It is in such a unity of love that the power for the miraculous is released. It is in the presence of such power that even people like the Sodom-ites, let alone world leaders, can begin wisdom in the fear of the Lord. Paramount in our teaching are unity of love and the power of the Holy Spirit. Fear is a major factor in the argument for nuclear deterrents, but perfect love casts out fear (1 Jn 4:8). The Spirit's power also gives ground for repentance and faith (1 Cor 2:4,5). With such weapons, nuclear weapons and their proponents may be challenged, and the latter called to repent.

Thirdly, Jesus rebukes the undisguised love of *vengeance*

that plagues human beings and has started many wars. It is natural to feel anger at the sin of others, but a desire for revenge goes against the Spirit of Jesus. 'The Son of Man came not to destroy people's lives, but to save them,' Jesus reminded them (Lk 9:55 margin). As God's people we need to deal with the root causes of strife and warfare as they exist in our own hearts and lives, so that we can truly be a people who make for peace.

This means that in our Fellowship the kind of ministry must be available which deals with inner hurts and broken spirits; spirits of anger, violence, uncleanness and fear must all be cast out. When bitterness and resentments have gone, bruised souls set free, and spirits unblocked, interior room is made in the believer. Those shepherding the flock must know that the inner lives of the people are filled with the riches of Christ's glory so that the growing disciples may be strengthened with might by Jesus' Spirit in their spirits. (Eph 3:16). Then God's people not only talk peace but live and breathe it, forgiving and being forgiven. Discipline in such fellowships is imperative and must be as stringent as it is loving, dealing with issues of unlove and disunity as well as of adultery, lies, or theft. Constant care and counselling are called for so that relationships both within our community, as well as with Christians elsewhere, are in good state and all differences are reconciled.

On a number of occasions we have refused to receive believers who would not seek reconciliation with others. This crime against the Body of Christ is a sin against its head who has reconciled all things to Himself. When the peace of God rules our hearts we are able to challenge the war-like values of the bomb, free from vengeance and venom in our hearts against its exponents. This means that if, as the Samaritans did to our Lord in Luke 9:53, we are refused in our offers and overtures, free from vengeance we turn to another situation or village. Love is still the exercise of our hearts if our lives are growing inwardly in the Spirit. There will be no need to hate those who reject us and maybe the next village will receive us and our objections and reasons. God is still at work while we pursue other people and directions to influence and perhaps like the Samaritans some seven years later (as in Acts 8), those who rejected us will receive our message of peace with rejoicing.

The Cost

Such Godly peace will be challenged, however. There are powerful forces of evil at work in the world. The Book of Revelation paints a dark and forceful picture of end-time warfare.

'Men worshipped the dragon because he had given authority to the beast, and they also worshipped the beast and asked, "Who is like the beast? Who can make war against him?" The beast was given a mouth to utter proud words and blasphemies and to exercise authority for forty-two months. He opened his mouth to blaspheme God and to slander His name and dwelling place and those who live in Heaven. He was given power to make war against the saints and to conquer them and he was given authority over every tribe, people, language, and nation. All inhabitants of the earth will worship the beast – all whose names have not been written in the Book of Life belonging to the Lamb that was slain from the creation of the world. He who has an ear let him hear. If anyone is to go into captivity, into captivity he will go. If anyone is to be killed with the sword with the sword he will be killed. This calls for patient endurance and faithfulness on the part of the saints.' (Rev 13:4–10).

In such a dark passage of totalitarian violence and oppression, the one ray of light is the word coming from our Saviour Himself, for no one else in Scripture uses this phrase: 'If any man has an ear, let him hear.' His voice is still heard even under such intolerable oppression. It strengthens the saints who, in faithfulness and endurance stand firm in peace when war envelops their very existence. 'Blessed are the peacemakers for they shall be called Sons of God', is still the word of our Lord even when opposition is monolithic, universal and total against our stand in faith for peace. His words are our encouragement until the last day when the Prince of Peace will come.

Mark Mills-Powell

Mark Mills-Powell can claim the best of the British evangelical tradition, even within his family line. He is descended from Thomas Fowell Buxton, the abolitionist. Mark's own vision for a gospel ministry, 'breaking the shackles of oppression', began to be born, ironically, while he attended Eton College. It also took him to visit Sojourners Community in Washington, DC in 1979. He returned, two years later, a married man, and was ordained in the Church of England.

Recovering the richness of the evangelical heritage, Mark shows how revival in our time will necessarily mean exposing the lie of the bomb and claiming Jesus' Lordship over all.

15: The Call to Revival

Mark Mills-Powell

Today the Lord is making it increasingly clear to His Church in this country that He is wanting to bring *revival* to our land again. He is putting it into the hearts of more and more individuals to pray and prepare earnestly for it. But what is revival? It is the outpouring of God's very life, His Spirit, onto whole communities of people, as they are convicted of sin and the need for God in their lives. The preconditions of revival, as the prophet says (Is 57:15), are a lowly spirit and a contrite heart, and a body of praying, believing intercessors. It can not be engineered by us. It is God's sovereign gift, given by Him in response to the humble fervent prayers of His people.[1]

The Lord says (Ex 3:9f), 'The cry of my people has come unto me . . . I will deliver them.' He waits now for the concerted heartfelt cry of His people to come unto Him, that He might deliver us and visit us afresh with His salvation. His arm is not shortened. He wants to do this. He simply waits for intercessors to go before Him and prepare the way in prayer. And when revival comes, it will not only affect the religious or 'spiritual' part of an individual. It will bring in its train *social transformation*.

An Evangelical Heritage

Under the inspiration of Charles Finney in the last century in the USA, the abolition of slavery was made central to the

[1] See Clifford Hill's lead article in *Prophecy Today*, vol. 1. no. 3 1985.

religious experience of repentance and conversion. It was impossible for a slave-owner, moving towards re-birth in Christ, not to be confronted with the sinfulness of involvement in the evil institution of slavery. At conversion, the slave-owner had to renounce his participation and set free the slaves over whom he had power. As a result, revival impacted its society profoundly – not in a spiritualized subsection of life, but rather on perhaps the most important social issue of the day.

The historian, Gilbert Barnes, has argued that the antislavery impulse in the US was rooted in the experience of the evangelical converts of the Second Great Awakening. Conversion was understood not so much as a religious experience as a turning to unselfishness and an orientation towards others. Christians were called to reflect the 'disinterested benevolence' of God in their relationships. This led to the founding of 'benevolent societies', as expressions of Christian love. These benevolent societies came, in time, to dominate the era.

Finney, 'immersed in Scripture and drawn throughout his life to the quest of holiness in his own heart and life, understood the spiritual sources of social regeneration; precisely because he saw the biblical connections between God's grace, individual accountability, and the covenants of righteousness'.[2] The way of Christ was conceived primarily as a way of love, service, and caring, and only secondarily as a matter of right belief and doctrine.

Finney's priorities can be mirrored in the lives and ministries of other evangelicals and evangelists from the last century. John Wesley understood clearly the implications of a full and whole conversion to Christ. He understood how the conformed, national church was its own worst enemy in proclaiming the Gospel. He understood that there was no New Testament basis for the wedding of the state with an established church and he apprehended it 'a mere political institution'. He decried the Constantinian settlement.

In contrast to the protected, safe and yet spiritually impotent position of the established church, his own revival

[2]Timothy L. Smith, *Sojourners* March 1984.

movement began in the midst of social unrest, turmoil and danger. He had been invited by George Whitefield to Bristol in 1739 after an uprising in the region had been suppressed by soldiers and imprisonments. He preached, on that first occasion, with a keen consciousness that he could be killed in the process. His audience was made up of 3,000 rough-hewn colliers and his text was: 'The Spirit of the Lord is upon me, because he has annointed me to preach good news to the poor . . .' (Lk 4:18f.). His open-air meetings were never safe affairs; they regularly suffered the accusation of illegality, in breach of the Conventicle Act.

He had no time for preaching a sermon that did not lead directly from a confession of faith to a charge for practical faithfulness in daily living. 'The General Rules of the United Societies' which he set up spell out the ethical obligations incumbent upon a new believer:

— 'No buying or selling of spirits or liquors or drinking them,
— No buying or selling of men, women and children with an intention to enslave them,
— No returning evil for evil,
— No putting on of gold or costly apparel,
— No laying up treasure on the earth.'

Conversion was meant to be signified by certain precise changes in the way in which the individual lived. The gospel had a social dimension as well as a spiritual one – or put another way, genuine spiritual change – conversion – always resulted in social upheaval and transformation.

Wesley himself was rigorously faithful to the direction of social change that he advocated in 'The General Rules of the United Societies'. By wearing the plainest apparel, making his own fire, fasting and stretching his meals, he saved almost half his annual income 'so that he had nearly £20 to return to God in the poor'. In one of his writings, *Works*, he states, 'I myself as well as the other preachers who are in town, diet with the poor on the same food, at the same table. And we rejoice herein as a comfortable earnest, of our eating bread together in our Father's kingdom.'

This evangelist, by the empowering of God's Holy Spirit, initiated a spiritual revival, which impacted its own society profoundly, by not *hiding* the cost of genuine discipleship, but rather, by *emphasizing* it.

The Test For Revival

Here then are just two examples from the evangelical tradition, of people who have sought to bear witness to the whole gospel, who have boldly outlined the social character of a spiritually renewed and transformed people. They have unequivocally claimed that to be truly converted involves taking sides on controversial issues of the day. They sought to make explicit the pain of a real spiritual re-birth and set their faces against phoney short-cuts. They were unpopular with the establishment, as the gospel they preached threatened the status quo and its hold over the people. Their message was good news, genuinely directed towards the poor, and their witness sought the liberation and release of those that were bound and oppressed.

The importance of the anti-slavery movement for us today is well expressed in a tract called, 'The New Abolitionist Covenant,' quoted here:

Some historical issues stand out as particularly urgent among the church's fundamental concerns. These over-arching moral questions intrude upon the routine of the church's life and plead for the compassion and courage of God's people everywhere. Slavery was such a question for Christians in the 19th century. The nuclear arms race is such a question today . . . Christian acceptance of nuclear weapons has brought us also to a crisis of faith. The nuclear threat is not just a political issue any more than slavery was: it is a question that challenges our worship of God and our commitment to Jesus Christ. In other words, the growing prospect of nuclear war presents us with more than a test of survival; it confronts us with a test of faith.'[3]

[3]*New Abolitionist Covenant*, published by 'Aslancrafts,' 86 Pottemewton Lane, Leeds LS7 3LW.

It is not sufficient to claim the fine tradition of Wesley and Finney in the 18th and 19th centuries as one's own, and at the same time pull back in fear from taking a similar stand today. It will mean courageously risking status or reputation, securities or jobs, as one dares to *apply* the gospel's message to our historical crisis. We draw back from being too explicit about what following Jesus Christ, the Prince of Peace, in the nuclear age will entail; and in so doing we reduce the gospel's reach. We are afraid of 'putting people off', wrongly thinking that the number of disciples matters more than the depth of discipleship – and so abandon Christ's example of focusing patiently and persistently on only twelve individuals for the best part of his three years of public ministry. We dilute the gospel call, and then wonder why Christians and the Christian Church have such little impact on our society. Jesus said to His followers, 'You are the salt of the earth', 'You are the light of the world'; but he also warned, 'If salt becomes tasteless, what can make it salty again? It is good for nothing, and can only be thrown out to be trampled underfoot.' (Mt. 5:13f.).

Bonhoeffer reminded us that when Jesus called his disciples, He bid them come and die. (cf Jn 12:24). We wriggle with embarrassment at having such a word to share, and ask to be excused the task, perhaps remembering the treatment prophets have nearly always received. It is so much easier to proclaim a gospel of prosperity and upward mobility. But the words of Jesus do not change, 'Whoever would come after me, let that person take up his (or her) cross and follow me . . .' (Mk 8:34f.).

An encounter with God in His power and purposefulness is seldom, if ever, comfortable. We fear what will be asked of us, the sacrifices required, the risks that must be undertaken. We are acutely aware of our own past failures and enduring frailty. When Isaiah beheld the Lord in His glory in the Temple 6:5 his response was, 'Woe is me! For I am a man of unclean lips, and I dwell in the midst of a people of unclean lips; and my eyes have seen the Lord.' (Is 6:5).

But the divine summons does not halt at that point: God does not just want to bring a spirit of penitence upon His people. He wants to make disciples. As we read on, we observe Isaiah overhearing the deliberations in heaven, 'Who will go for us?' (v. 8); and he responds, 'Lord, here I am, send me'. He puts himself in the position where his life will be changed by God and brought into line with His all-wise purposes. Are we in danger today of succumbing to the temptation of proclaiming a gospel which calls people to a sense of sorrow for their past failures without also inviting them into the costly path of discipleship? 'Follow me', says Jesus; and we read that they left their nets and followed Him (Mark 1:18).

The Need For Revival

In the past forty years in this country we have experienced some strong, large-scale evangelistic efforts; but, I believe, the time is coming when God wants to give us genuine mass revival. Though the one helps to prepare for the latter, it is as nothing compared to the power of God, which is made manifest in Revival. The historian, J. Wesley Bready in *England: Before and After Wesley*, claims that the evangelical revival of the eighteenth century 'did more to transfigure the moral character of the general populace, than any other movement British history can record'.[4] The revival swept through the land and changed the face of the nation. Bestiality and inhumanity gave way to compassion and reforming zeal, corruption to desire for honesty and uprightness, exploitation to a commitment to protect the weak. Historian after historian documents the remarkable transformation which took place in the life of the nation. 'As Professor Harold Perkin states in his recent book on the period, 'between 1780 and 1850 the English ceased to be one of the most aggressive, brutal, rowdy, outspoken, riotous, cruel and bloodthirsty nations in the world and became one of the most inhibited, polite, orderly, tender-minded, prudish and hypocritical'. The evidence of this transition is clear throughout every level of society.'[5] God intervened in

---

[4] J. Wesley Bready, *England: Before & After Wesley*, p. 327; Hodder & Stoughton, 1939.
[5] Ian Bradley, *The Call to Seriousness*, Jonathan Cape Ltd, 1976.

response to the cries of His people, and transformed, by His gracious sovereign power, the life of a nation.

Today our plight is no less serious, and perhaps worse, than the Britain of the early eighteenth century. Institutional-ized injustice has become a way of life for our nation and those of the 'developed' world. Our resources are channelled towards weapons of war and ever more advanced military technology to the tragic neglect of those who flounder in despair and bitterness in our inner-cities and impoverished council estates, let alone the other two-thirds of the world. Church attendance has declined to a tiny fraction of the population (approximately 5%, far less than the Soviet Union), and how many of those have any vision for what God could do through His church is uncertain.

We lie in a desperate plight; and, even more dangerously, are often totally blind to our waywardness and the impending judgment, which is only restrained by God's enduring mercy. 'As it was in the days of Noah, so it will be in the days of the Son of Man. They ate, they drank, they married, they were given in marriage, until the day when Noah entered the ark and the flood came and destroyed them all . . . so will it be on the day when the Son of Man is revealed.' (Lk 17:26, 30). Dale Aukerman comments on these verses,

> 'The wickedness and the forces that impel the world toward doom are mostly out of sight or not recognized for what they are. Few see even partially with God in His seeing (as the Hebrew prophets did). Most human beings live out day after day absorbed in consumption, production, commerce, self-gratification. And each such day moves inevitably on – unless there is a human turning around – toward that day which will be overwhelmingly unlike all the ordinary days preceding it, that day of sudden inundating cataclysm, that day of fire and worse than brimstone raining across continents.'[6]

. . . Unless there is a human turning around. Though our

[6]Dale Aukerman, *Darkening Valley*, p. 154, SPCK, 1982.

plight is terrible, God is more than able to intervene, save us, and turn us to his pathways of righteousness and of justice.

A Corporate Sin

But part of our turning around must be the ready acknowledgement that we have done wrong to stockpile nuclear weapons of mass destruction, targeting, among others, our brother and sister Christians in Soviet Russia. We must acknowledge again that the Kingdom of God cannot be defended, protected, or extended by physical force ('Not by might, nor by power, but by my Spirit' says the Lord of Hosts,' Zech 4:6) and that to continue to trust in such weapons for our security is to deny our faith in God.

Such action is part of the preparation necessary for what God in His great graciousness wants to bring to us: revival. Charles Finney recognized that neglect of such matters hindered the work of revival;[7] and the evangelical historian of the period, Donald Dayton, has written, 'the agitation (that is, the anti-slavery agitation in the U.S.A.) . . . prompted by an impulse religious in character and evangelical in spirit . . . *began* the Great Revival of 1830.[8] As we confront this issue in the Spirit of God (and the other areas of unrighteousness He lays on our heart to address) we actually help to prepare the way for revival. To engage this issue is not to become side-tracked; it is to quicken God's blessing and forward His purposes of restoration and deliverance.

Ronald Sider, the American evangelical author has written:

Let's pray for a mighty revival that brings millions of sinners into a living personal relationship with Jesus Christ. Let's pray for a revival that restores millions of lukewarm church members. Let's pray that the Holy Spirit leads those transformed by revival to join the Prince of Peace in a worldwide crusade for the abolition of nuclear

[7]Charles Finney, 23rd Lecture on Revival cited in *Issues facing Christians Today*, John Stott, p. 5, Marshalls, 1984.
[8]Donald W. Dayton, *Sojourners* (formerly *Post-American*) March 1975.

weapons. Let's pray for a peace revival in which people see that Jesus is the only way to peace and that peace is the way of Jesus. Let's pray that Evangelicals, because they have a personal relationship with the Prince of Peace, will take the lead in answering His call, 'Blessed are the peacemakers.'[9]

What we will do if we are faithful in this matter is to create the opportunity for God to visit us with a revival which will engender repentance and beckon all away from the idols of destruction and towards the Lord and Giver of Life, Jesus Christ. John Haughton has said:

'The nuclear arms race is a Satanic attempt to foil the spread of the Kingdom of God and to prevent the return of Jesus for His bride. . . . The Devil will try to oppose it by every means at his disposal. . . . Part of our spiritual warfare must be to pray against the rise of nuclear weapons. You don't have to sort out whether you are a unilateralist or a multilateralist. You have just got to be opposed to this Satanic work.'[10]

Why? Because God has given us time to pray and to work for the fulfilment of His purposes for the end of the age.

But is our vision fixed on the Lamb upon the throne (as described in Rev 5:8–14) who is the end-point unto whom this world is evolving? Will we recognize the One who is to be lifted up as the banner, the ensign, and the standard in the next world revival? Or, are we distracted, unsure where to focus?

That Lamb inherits the Kingdom, not only because he has been God's Son from the beginning. He reigns because He was slain and by His blood He has ransomed all people for God. For God to accomplish His purposes in Christ we must give up flirting with the supposed security that nuclear weapons offer us, which is the Devil's masquerade, his lie.

[9]Ronald Sider, *The Plough*, Journal of Hutterian Society of Brothers, November 1983.
[10]John Haughton at Downs Bible Week, *Kingdom Matters* Tape no. 4, Coastlands Cassettes.

If he succeeds in fooling us, it will assuredly result in our destruction. 'If you eat of this fruit, you will become like God,' Satan says; while God's final judgement is death, 'If you eat of this fruit, you shall surely die.' (Gen 3:5; 3:3).

Total death and destruction are not inevitable, though as we are becoming increasingly aware[11] they are a distinct possibility. God holds out to us the offer of repentance. Again and again He has delayed judgement on our behalf, simply because He loves us and desires that not one should perish. He says to us incessantly, earnestly, 'Now is the time to repent and seek my face! I have extended time for you in the past by averting the complete eclipse of the human race in the Flood; by sending my prophets to you down the ages, I have warned you of danger and the possibility of repentance. My arms are still outstretched towards you, waiting for you to turn, waiting for you to come back to me, and leave these weapons of destruction behind. Now is the time to repent and come to me.'

If we turn to God, allowing Him to shape us into true disciples, He will deliver us from the clutches of death and lead us into the most glorious revival this world has ever known. In it we will rediscover Jesus as the Prince of Peace, the One who is to receive all power, wealth, wisdom, might, glory, and blessing, both now and forever.

[11]See Sidney Lens, *The Day Before Doomsday*, Beacon Press, Boston, 1977.

Marian Landis

Some people become involved in the peace movement, others are born into it. Marian Landis, who comes from a Mennonite background in the US, would admit that while belonging to a church historically opposed to war, she had to decide what being a peacemaker would mean for herself. Now based at the London Mennonite Centre and just returned from a year's sabbatical spent at seminary in Elkhart, Indiana, she will pick up her involvements with Evangelical Peacemakers and Christian CND as part of her work for peace.

It is fitting that we should close with Marian's chapter on the hope which we who will follow Jesus must claim for our journey.

16: Believing Against All Hope

Marian Landis

The following article originally appeared in the MCC Peace Section Newsletter, Vol XV, No. 3, May–June 1985. Reproduced by permission.

'Peacemakers must be the most optimistic people in the world to try making a dent in the problems,' said a Christian acquaintance recently.

I fell to thinking about that, and I think he has it wrong. I don't think peacemakers, at least not Christian peacemakers, are the most optimistic people in the world. Perhaps I should only say that I am not. In fact, in the last six years or so, during which I've been involved in 'peace work full-time' (whatever that means), my optimism has steadily eroded until I identify with Dan Berrigan, who said, 'There are no longer any grounds at all for optimism.'

Perhaps it is partly because we know too much. Our worldwide news coverage ensures that we know the worst that is happening everywhere, almost as soon as it happens. It is more than we can bear, if we choose to listen. 'I long to take my bundle of knowledge and pitch it overboard,' wrote a friend not long ago. I understand well.

But I think our lack of optimism springs from something deeper. We as human beings now have a knowledge and ability of a most terrible sort, that which can destroy the earth and humanity and history as we have known it within a matter of seconds. Having to face the awareness that our drive to create and change has led to that kind of invention must surely cause us to concede: 'There are no longer grounds at all for optimism.'

Another way of looking at it: the Bomb shows with irresistible clarity what has been true all along: we are utterly out of our depths as peacemakers.

The Bomb shows, perhaps as never before in history, that the way out cannot lie in propping up our dying optimism with yet another invention, yet another attempt at reform. We cannot dis-invent nuclear weapons, nor can we by our own effort dismantle that of the Bomb which lies within each one of us. (If we are honest, we must recognize and accept the intimate connection between the two.)

Rather, the way out lies in facing our bankruptcy as peacemakers in both our inner and outer landscapes, and then like Job upon hearing of the calamities which took away all his apparent sources of security, falling down to worship. Only then do we begin to find hope, which in contrast to optimism, enables us to dare to take on the task of peacemaking in a world gone grey in the long dark shadow of nuclear annihilation.

How does this hope come to be? The words used to describe Abraham in Romans 4:18 and 19 (NIV) aptly fit our contemporary struggle to experience hope. 'Against all hope, Abraham in hope believed. . . . Without weakening in his faith, he faced the fact that his body was as good as dead. . . .' Only several hours' worth of research into the capability of our nuclear weapons in 1985 reveals that we too are as good as dead. This is a fearful thing to face. There are days when I lack the courage to think about it; it is too painful. Earlier today, when I fled to the heath for a couple of hours, I found myself looking at the magnificent sweep of greening earth and aching with longing that we not burn it up. But hope must first look at things as they are; it cannot pitch its bundle of knowledge overboard.

Yet perhaps the long grey shadow of nuclear annihilation is not, in fact, the most difficult reality to face. I am coming to think that it is not. At least I am finding it just as difficult, if not more, to face the long grey shadow within me, my own participation in destructivity. I too, am fearful, greedy, violent, dying. I find it enormously preferable to ignore those elements within me. But to do so is not only to hide the truth and thus disallow hope for change, it is also to be in danger of projecting that which we find unacceptable within ourselves on to another and labelling that person or group the evil one, the enemy.

This then, paradoxically, is where hope starts, at the point of seeming hopelessness. But the Good News is that we need not, dare not, remain there. Like Abraham who turned from the deadness of his body to the promise of God, we have been called from our deadness – the impossibility of our living in peace – to the promise and act of God.

What was Abraham's hope? That of having a son? Not ultimately. It was full persuasion that God had power to do what he had promised. What am I hoping? That the Bomb will never be used? That a weapon of some sort will keep my death at bay? Such apparent sources of security are as tempting to lean upon and put my primary commitment to as leaning upon Isaac for security must have tempted Abraham.

Children are blessings, particularly the child Isaac, born miraculously. Nuclear disarmament is good, and I long and pray for it. Prolonging and improving the quality of my life seems important. But none of these is strong enough ultimately to bear the weight of our need for security. Depending on such leads only to anxious swings of optimism and pessimism, of activism and withdrawal, but not to hope, and its capacity for sustained trust and involvement.

Just as the promise and act of God, not Isaac himself, was ultimately Abraham's hope (this difference was put to an excruciating test), so we find our hope finally in nothing other than the nature of God, who as both Creator and Lover has chosen to act savingly on our behalf, becoming also our Redeemer.

The Good News is that the shattered beauty of ourselves and all of creation is to be restored, not discarded. The hateful places within us, broken relationships among us, scarred creation around us, are to be set free to be that which our Creator intended in the first place. This is perhaps what moves me most about the Gospel: I who for many years (even as a Christian) considered my essential self of dubious worth at best, now discover that not only am I not to be destroyed, I am offered healing and freedom to become who I am meant to be. My pain, my wounds, my lame places – all that lurks under my long grey shadow – are to be *redeemed*. We are to live in relationships of wholeness with our Creator; and ourselves, our fellow humans, and the natural world around us. Unexpectedly, I am finding the utter loss of optimism embodied in the bomb to be metamorphosing into a new understanding of the astonishing miracle of this hope.

Not division and discarding (the bomb discards all), but healing and inclusion. This is the nature of hope, endlessly outgoing. (It is characteristic of love, to hope *all things*.) As hope begins to flow into us, we find ourselves taking on its inclusive character. Love your enemies. Welcome the stranger. Give to those who ask of you. The qualities of peacemaking: we are the recipients of them, and now they become possible for us. We find ourselves, in fact, going back to the very places where we have experienced most deeply the desolation of our personal power to make peace – our dying optimism – and practising hope there, in both our inner and outer worlds.

Within, we find that we no longer are paralyzed by the questions: am I lovable? can I be saved from the nothingness of death? We have been given a yes that is even more discernible than that given to Abraham. Not that we never ask the questions again, but the fearful, deadly preoccupation is gone.

This yes is simultaneously expressed in the outer world of all our relationships, involvements, encounters. Hope denies its own nature if this is not so. It is not an automatic, effortless kind of hope-incarnating, however. No longer insensible in the flat deadness of the grey shadow, we now begin to feel the full texture and colour of the human journey, with all its pain and possibility. Rather than escaping from the world, we find ourselves called, like Jesus, to live *in it*. The hope given us prevails, not by trivializing or deserting the world of human failure and distress, but by taking that into its life.

So we are called to live in a strange place – between the tension of a hope that is sure, and yet not completely seen;

between Abraham's sacrifice of his son Isaac, and his father-hood of many nations; between the agony of the cross, and the joy of the empty grave.

Or between the bomb and the ploughed field, I say to myself. I am thinking of a cold, windswept day in May last year, when our small Fellowship and a few friends gathered outside a huge nuclear base in England to worship. As the wind tore at our coats and froze our fingers, we sang, prayed, meditated, shared communion, and planted a tree. I remember thinking about the enormous new nuclear bunker behind the barbed wire fence beside us, feeling horrified at the presence of the bomb. Then as we turned to plant our small, vulnerable, beautiful apple tree, our eyes fastened on the magnificent ploughed field across from us, on the other side of the road edging the base. I remember feeling great joy at the sight of the rich, upturned earth with its prospect of life-giving harvest, its clear stamp of the Creator. We turned towards it, as if acting out the choice we were articulating in our worship together. The joy remains. Yet the ache of the contradiction – that bombs should exist beside ploughed fields – does not go away either.

It is into this tension – the intersections of the human experience between life-defying and life-giving forces – that we are called to plant trees, practice hope, make peace – to *worship*. And although we are called to this in all places where fear scars life, sometimes I think that the presence of the bomb – whether literally in a factory or on a base, or vicariously through the diversion of resources – renders to us a particularly desperate call for the specific, creative, redemptive attention of worshipping Christians.

There is a patch of wheat growing on the Ministry of Defense land of Molesworth, the airbase in idyllic Cambridgeshire where sixty-four American cruise missiles are to be placed by 1988. This wheat is destined for hungry people in Ethiopia. It was planted last autumn by Christians and others who grieved that the purpose of Molesworth's 630 acres of fertile earth should be so profaned as to become the storing and launching place of nuclear weapons.

There is also a small peace chapel on a corner of Moles-worth. It was built by volunteers, stone by stone, from ugly chunks of tarmac which had been thrown on a peace garden nearby. The tarmac originally came from an old runway on the base. Although the chapel is not finished, it has been a gathering point for many Christians and others who have come there to worship and pray for peace.

It is possible that the wheat may never be harvested, and the chapel never finished. For they both now exist behind a 7½-mile-long, 6-foot-high barbed wire fence, suddenly and stealthily erected around the formerly relative inactive base by the Ministry of Defence one snowy night in February, a sign that active preparations for the arrival of cruise missiles were beginning, and that 'peace protestors' should hence-forth discard their hope for the reclamation of Molesworth.

But those audacious gestures of hope – of reclaiming our choice of bread instead of bombs, worship instead of oblivion – have not been fenced away, out of reach. They cannot be. Indeed, they are multiplying. Inspired by the wheat growing on nuclear base land, people are gathering in other grain to send to Ethiopia – much more, in fact, than the acres sown on Molesworth can produce. Seeing the image of the peace chapel behind the barbed wire fence, more people are beginning to think, pray, and act against nuclear weapons. More people, not fewer, are focusing on Molesworth, to continue to try to reclaim its life-giving potential.

II Corinthians 3:12 says that 'since we have such a hope, we are very bold'. We, who are seeing the death of opti-mism, now view with less clouded eyes the extraordinary redemption that has been extended to us in the incarnation of Jesus. Let us, rooted in that matchless audacity of hope, live out our hope with holy, creative boldness.

For more information about Evangelical Peacemakers in the U.K., contact one of the following:

SCOTLAND

Glasgow: Eric MacArthur, 4 Alexander Terrace, Neilston, Renfrewshire 041–881–3924.

Edinburgh: Bob Marsh, Flat 7, 19 West Micholson Street, Edinburgh EH8 9DA 031–668 2268.

Aberdeen: David Smith, 19 Forvie Terrace, Bridge of Don, Aberdeen AB2 8TH

ENGLAND

Durham: Mark Pritchard, 79a Front Street, Sherburn Village, Durham City DH6 1HD 0385–721761.

Newcastle-on-Tyne: Richard and Carol Evans, 40 Balmoral Terrace, South Gosforth, Newcastle-on-Tyne NE3 1YH 091–284 5980.

North Yorkshire: Colin Pratt, 8 Orchard Way, Selby, N. Yorks 0757–706158.

Leeds: Sue Hilton, 37 Wilton Grove, Leeds 6 Leeds 787646.

Hull: Jack and Ann Snowdon, 59 Birklands Drive, Hull HU8 0L9 N. Humberside 0482–796639

Bradford: George Crossley, 22 Yarwood Grove, Bradford BD7 4RN

Greater Manchester: Martin and Jean Tullet, 201 Anglia House, Gardenia Square, Ardwick, Manchester M1Z 4AF

Cumbria: Audrey Greenwood, 87 Hurley Road, Little Corby, Carlisle, Cumbria CA4 8QY

Merseyside: Colin and Rose Ross, 51 Calthorpe Street, Garston, Liverpool 051–427 5145
Frank and Pam Naylor, 27 Daresbury Road, Eccleston, St. Helens St. Helens 57034.

Wolverhampton: Alister Palmer, 27 Morrison Avenue, Bushbury, Wolverhampton WV10 9TS 0902–734648.

Walsall: Dr. H. K. Beardwood, 1 Woodside Way, Aldridge, Walsall, W. Midlands WS9 0HY Aldridge 52742

Birmingham: Chris Walton, 200 Monument Road, Edgbaston, Birmingham 16 8UU 021–455 7271.

Worcester and Hereford: Vaughan Stillman, 12 Yates Hay Road, Malvern Link, Malvern, Worcs.

Gloucester: Arthur and Ursula Windsor, 4 Brunswick Square, Gloucester GL1 1HG 0452–21184.

Nottingham: Arthur Ashe, St. John's College, Bramcote, Nottingham.

Northants: Simon and Elaine Beard, 28 William Street, Burton Latimer, Kettering, Northants 0536–724192.

East Anglia: Nigel Parfitt, 137 Spencer Street, Norwich, Norfolk 0603–483953.

Cambridge: Vivienne Faull, Chaplain, Clare College, Cambridge.

Herts: Simon Curran, 39 Ward Crescent, Bishops Stortford, Herts. CM23 3QR.

West Country: Roger and Joyce Tyler, Dennings, Wallingford Road, Kingsbridge, Devon 0548–3287.

Southwest: Andrew Gough, 43 Hazeldene Road, Patchway, Bristol BS12 5DT

Dorset and Wilts: Edward Cardale, Vicarage, Lytchett Minster, Poole, Dorset.

South: (Berks, Hants, Isle of Wight): Rob Collins, 12 Upper Crown Street, Reading, Berks RG1 2SS 0734–862579.

London:

North: Will Newcomb, London Mennonite Centre, 14 Shepherds Hill, Highgate, London N6 5AQ 01–340 8775.

East: Helen Rigby, 20 Ridley Road, Forest Gate, London E7 0LT 01–534 2199.

West: Gill and Trevor Scott, 1 Woodgrange Avenue, Ealing, London W5. 01–992 5715

South: Andy Vail, 28 Hillcross Avenue, Morden, Surrey SM4 4EA 01–540 6750.

Southeast: Lindi Carter, 264 Barnett Wood Lane, Ashtead, Surrey 03722–767

NORTHERN IRELAND: David Anderson, 17 Victoria Way, Dungannon, Co. Tyrone, No. Ireland BT71 7AD 86–22880.

WALES:
Arfon Jones, Penyberth, 76 Glenwood, Llanedeyrn, Cardiff CF2 6UT
or Tony Rudman, 29 Commercial Road, Newport, Gwent.

CENTRAL ADMINISTRATOR: Stuart Hemsley, 59 Harold Street, Hereford HR1 2QU Hereford 55724.

THEOLOGICAL SUPPORT GROUP:
The Rev. Graham Cray, St. Michael-le-Belfry, St. Cuthberts Centre, Peasholme Green, York YO1 2PW

Mr Jim Punton, Frontier Youth Trust, 130 City Road, London EC1

The Rev. Chris Sugden, Oxford Centre for Mission Studies, St. Philip and St. James' Church, Woodstock Road, Oxford.

The Rt. Rev. Peter Hall, Bishop of Woolwich, 8B Hillyfields Crescent, Brockley, London SE4 1QA

Dss. June Osborne, 37 Ellesmere Road, Bow, London E3

Mr Rob Warner, 29 Poplar Close, Kidlington, Oxford.

Dr. Alan Kreider, London Mennonite Centre, 14 Shepherds Hill, Highgate, London N6 5AQ

The Rev. Andrew Kirk, London Institute for Contemporary Christianity, St. Peter's Vere Street, London W1

Ms. Jeanne Hinton, Little Chimneys, Lytchett Minster, Poole, Dorset.

Dana and Mark Mills-Powell, Huyton Parish Church, Bluebell Lane, Huyton, Liverpool 36 7XE (Until 1986).

For Further Reading

★ Aldridge, Robert, *First Strike*: The Pentagon's Strategy for Nuclear War, South End Press, Boston, 1983.

The Alternative Defence Commission, *Defence Without the Bomb*, Taylor and Francis Ltd, London, 1983.

★ Aukerman, Dale, *Darkening Valley*: A Biblical Perspective on Nuclear War, Seabury Press (SPCK), New York, 1981.

The Church of England Working Party, *The Church and the Bomb*, Hodder and Stoughton, London, 1982.

Committee on Poverty and the Arms Trade, *Bombs for Breakfast*, COPAT, London, 1978.

Dando, Malcolm and Paul Rogers, *The Death of Deterrence*, CND, London, 1983.

Ellul, Jacques, *Violence*, Seabury Press, New York, 1969.

Freedman, Lawrence, *The Evolution of Nuclear Strategy*, MacMillan, 1983.

Hershey, John, *Hiroshima*, Knopf, New York, 1946.

Kirk, Andrew, *A New World Coming*: A Fresh Look at the Gospel for Today, Marshall, Morgan and Scott, Basingstoke, 1983.

★ Kreider, Alan, *Social Holiness*, Marshall Pickering, Basingstoke, 1986.

Ramsey, Paul, *The Just War*, University Press of America, 1983.

Sider, Ron and Richard Taylor, *Nuclear Holocaust and Christian Hope*, Hodder and Stoughton, London, 1982.

A. Sivanandan, *A Different Hunger*: Writings on Black Resistance, Pluto Press.

Sugden, Chris, *Radical Discipleship*, Marshall, Morgan and Scott, Basingstoke, 1981.

Time to Choose: A Grassroots Study Guide on the Nuclear Arms Race, Celebration Services, Poole, Dorset, 1983.

★ Wallis, Jim, *Waging Peace*, Harper and Row, San Francisco, 1982.
★   ,,   ,   ,,   , *Peacemakers*, Harper and Row, San Francisco, 1983.
     ,,   ,   ,,   , *The Call to Conversion*, Lion, Tring, Herts, 1982.
Ann Wilkinson, *It's Not Fair*, Christian Aid, London.
★ Yoder, John Howard, *The Politics of Jesus*, Eerdmans, Grand Rapids, MI, 1972.
★   ,,   ,   ,,   ,,   *The Original Revolution*, Herald Press, Scottdale, PA, 1971.

★ Available from Metanoia Books, 14 Shepherds Hill, London N6 5AQ